DEVOTIONS
FOR THE
CHILDREN'S HOUR

Books by Kenneth N. Taylor

THE BIBLE IN PICTURES FOR LITTLE EYES
DEVOTIONS FOR THE CHILDREN'S HOUR
I SEE
A LIVING LETTER FOR THE CHILDREN'S HOUR
STORIES FOR THE CHILDREN'S HOUR
THE LIVING NEW TESTAMENT (*Tyndale House Publishers*)
LIVING PROPHECIES (*Tyndale House Publishers*)
LIVING PSALMS AND PROVERBS (*Tyndale House Publishers*)

DEVOTIONS FOR THE CHILDREN'S HOUR

by KENNETH N. TAYLOR

Illustrated by ROBERT G. DOARES

MOODY PRESS • CHICAGO

DEVOTIONS FOR THE CHILDREN'S HOUR. *Copyright © 1954, 1968, 1982 by Kenneth N. Taylor. Manufactured in the United States of America. All rights reserved.*

Library of Congress Catalog Card Number:
ISBN: 0-8024-0061-2

99 100 101 102 103 104 Printing/LC/Year 88 87 86 85 84 83

Contents

A Note to Mother and Dad

THIS IS NOT a Bible storybook. It is a book of doctrine for children—a book that tells what the Bible says about sin, and heaven, and about the Lord Jesus, and many other major Bible themes.

It is a book written especially for children: its words are simple and its thoughts, we hope, are clear.

There are many Bible storybooks, but children need doctrine, too, and books of doctrine written so children can understand have been until now almost unknown. But children need to understand what the Bible teaches as well as to hear its wonderful true stories. The truth and meaning of the stories must be combined with all else the Bible says, and the result stated simply and briefly and interestingly.

It is believed that this book will be understood by children as young as six years of age, and that it will be of continuing interest to children through the eleventh year.

This book goes hand in hand with any good Bible storybook. Both are necessary. Neither one alone is enough. And neither one is a satisfactory substitute for the Bible itself. Primary children can usually read the gospel of Mark or John if there is family encouragement.

But while the child is learning to read the Scriptures, he also needs to have the great Bible truths building up within him as pivots or centers around which all that he reads can relate.

A child thus fortified can withstand many a frightening intellectual assault in coming years. The truths of the Scriptures become to him familiar friends rather than misty figures and vague acquaintances who can help little in time of need.

The Word of God is a strong tonic and tower. In this book that Word is stated for the children. The meat of the Word is cut up fine so that children can eat it; but it is still meat—good, solid food on which anyone can be nourished.

It is suggested that one chief use of the book may well be as part of the daily family altar. Another, called to our attention by many readers of the first printing, is for Sunday school teachers and children's church leaders.

A word of explanation should be made to some parents in regard to the prayers that accompany each daily reading. These may be easily omitted by those who do not wish to make use of them, or who feel that written prayers are not proper; but it is hoped that others who do not have such reservations will find them helpful. In no case should they be considered as adequate for family worship. In addition, there should be prayer by each member of the household at the close of the devotional period.

These lessons should be used more than once. Spurgeon tells us that in planting beans the old practice was to put three in each hole; one for the worm, one for the crow, and one to live and produce a crop. In teaching children we must give line upon line and precept upon precept, repeating the truth which we would teach until it becomes impossible for the child to forget.

NOTE: The suggested Bible readings will be much more helpful and meaningful to both children and adults if read from a modern version, available from any bookstore.

1

There Is Only One God

IN SOME COUNTRIES where the people don't have Bibles and don't know very much about God, they think that there are several gods. Some of them think there are two gods, some think there are four gods and some of them think there are even a hundred gods or more. Or, they may think that the sun and the moon are gods, so they bow down and pray to the sun and moon. They ask the sun and moon to take care of them and help them.

Can the sun or the moon help us? No, these do not have life, they are not persons who can help us. They are only things that God has made to give us light, to keep us warm, and for us to enjoy. They are not gods, but they are made by

11

God. We should never pray to things that God has made, but only to God Himself.

Should we pray to the angels? Are they gods? No! The angels are alive, and there are some of them right here in the room (though we can't see them), but we shouldn't pray to them because they aren't gods. They are helpers and that is why God made them. The angels love God and there are so many of them that we cannot even think how many there are. Most of them are in heaven thanking and praising God and telling Him how glad they are to serve Him. But some of them are down here on earth helping us.

Up there in heaven are there any other gods except our God? No, God has made everything there is, and He did not make any other gods. That is why He is angry with those who pray to anyone but Himself. He is also angry with anyone who loves anything more than God. We must love God even more than we love our mothers and daddies and the nice things we have. For God gave us our mothers and daddies and all the other nice things. That is why we must love God best.

One day a minister wanted to know if a little girl knew that there was only one God. He said to her, "Katherine, how many gods are there?"

She said, "Only one."

"How do you know that?" asked the minister.

"Because," the little girl said to the minister, "there is only room enough for one God. He fills the heaven and the earth."

And the little girl was right.

SOMETHING TO READ FROM THE BIBLE: Exodus 20:1-6

QUESTIONS:

1. How many gods are there?

12

2. Can the sun or the moon hear us when we pray?
3. Should we pray to the angels? Are they gods?

A PRAYER:

Our heavenly Father, we thank You that You are the one and only God, that You are greater than anything else up in heaven or down here on the earth. Help us to love You with all of our hearts, and to serve only You. This we ask in Jesus' name. Amen.

A HYMN TO SING:

> All hail the power of Jesus' name
> Let angels prostrate fall;
> Bring forth the royal diadem,
> And crown Him Lord of all!
> Bring forth the royal diadem,
> And crown Him Lord of all!

2

Who Is God?

THERE ARE MANY THINGS we need to know. We need to know how to read and write; we need to know about arithmetic and social studies. But there is something much more important than reading and writing and arithmetic and social studies. Can you think what that most important thing is? I will tell you. It is to know about God. This is so important because God made you, and if you don't know about God, you won't know what He wants you to do.

Who is God? God is a Person who lives in a lovely place called heaven. We do not know just where heaven is, but we think it is far above the stars. It is a place where all of us would like to live, and if we know God and love Him, then

14

we can go to be with God and the angels when we die. That is another important reason for knowing about God.

Shall I tell you some more things about Him? Do you know that God is a Spirit? This means a Person without a body. You and I have bodies with our spirits inside them, but God does not need a body.

God is truly the most wonderful Person there is. He is kind and good. He never, never does a wrong thing. And He is so great that He can do anything He wants to. He made the world and the grass and the sky and the sun and the moon and the stars. He made the angels, and He made you and me. He made everything. He sends the thunder and the lightning and the rain. When the springtime comes with beautiful flowers and blue skies, it is because God makes it so.

Where is God? We have already learned that God is in the beautiful country of heaven, but God is also here in this room listening to us talk. He is next door, too. Isn't it strange that God can be here in our house and at the same time can be next door? He is everywhere! He is with the missionaries in other countries and with the people in the big ships on the ocean. We can only be one place at a time, but God is everywhere all at the same time.

One of the most important things for us to remember is that this great God is always loving us and always watching to see what we are doing. That should make us very glad, and it should make us careful about the things we do. We would not want to do anything God doesn't like. We know that our great God in heaven is always seeing us and helping us to do good things.

One day a man wanted to steal some watermelons from a field and took his little boy with him. The little boy was eight years old. His father told him to stand near the fence and watch to see if anyone was looking. While his father was in the field getting the watermelons, the little boy suddenly called out, "Daddy, Someone is watching you."

The man came running back to his little boy. "Where?" he asked. "Who is watching? Where is he?"

"Daddy," said the little boy, "when you were looking to see whether anyone could see you, you forgot to look up into the sky. God is looking down and watching you."

The little boy's father had never thought about that and decided not to steal watermelons anymore. The little boy was a good helper to his father because he reminded his father about God.

SOMETHING TO READ FROM THE BIBLE: Isaiah 6:1-8

QUESTIONS:

1. Does God have a body like you have?
2. Can you think of at least two places where God is, right now?
3. Can God see us at night when it is dark?

A PRAYER:

O God in heaven, holy God, forgive us for our many sins for we are often bad. We thank You that You forgive us through Jesus Christ our Lord. Amen.

A HYMN TO SING:

> Come, Thou Almighty King,
> Help us Thy name to sing,
> Help us to praise:
> Father, all glorious,
> O'er all victorious,
> Come, and reign over us,
> Ancient of Days.

3

Where Did God Come From?

THERE ARE MANY wonderful things about God that we cannot understand. We have already learned one of those things. We have learned that God can be everywhere at the same time. How strange this seems; we cannot understand how that can be at all! God has not explained this to us. When we get to heaven, He will tell us all about it, and then we will know.

There is something else about God that we cannot understand. To tell you what this other thing is, I am going to ask you a question. Where did God come from? Did He have a father and mother? No, God did not need a father and mother. He was never born. He was never a little child in heaven who grew up. He was not born in heaven because He has always been alive. He has always been great and wonderful, just exactly the same as He is now. He has always been alive.

God was alive yesterday, and the day before that, and the day before that. He was alive before you were born and before Mother and Daddy were born. He was alive before Grandfather was born and before there were any rocks and trees and grass and animals. He was alive millions and millions of years ago, before anything else happened.

Who made God? No one did. God was not made by anyone. God has always been alive. We cannot understand this, but we know that it is true.

God is always going to be alive.

Even little children should know that they will always be alive, too. That is the way God has made us. We will not always live here on earth. Some day our bodies will grow old and we will go away to live in another place. We can go then and live with God if we have been loving Him while we live here on earth with Mother and Daddy and our friends. We must learn to love God very much.

Some foolish people spend their time here on earth loving themselves instead of loving God. When they die, God will not want them in heaven but will send them away into a dark, sad place where they must live without God forever.

If we are going to live forever, then we must be very careful how we live now. But I am going to tell you a story about a rich farmer who forgot that he had to live forever.

This farmer went out to his barn and saw that it was full of grain. He went to another barn that he owned, and it was full of grain too. This made him very happy because he had so much grain in his barns. He knew he could sell the grain for a lot of money and that it would make him very rich.

"Oh," he said to himself, "now I will not need to work anymore. Now I will have a lot of money to buy plenty of whiskey and to eat more food than I should and to do all kinds of bad things."

When the farmer went to bed that night, he was still thinking about how rich he was and how he would spend his money, but he didn't think at all about what God wanted him to do with the money.

That night the rich farmer died. He had to meet God, and it was too late to remember then that God had wanted him to love the Lord Jesus and use his money to do good things and to tell others about Jesus.

I hope you will remember that you will always be alive, and I hope you will not be like the foolish rich man.

SOMETHING TO READ FROM THE BIBLE: Luke 12:16-28

QUESTIONS:

1. Was God ever born?
2. Was God alive before there were rocks and trees?
3. How long has God been alive?
4. How long will you be alive after your body dies?

A PRAYER:

Our Father in heaven, we thank You for giving us eternal life through Jesus Christ our Lord. Help us today to do the things that will please You. This we ask in Jesus' name. Amen.

A HYMN TO SING:

When we all get to heaven,
What a day of rejoicing that will be!
When we all see Jesus,
We'll sing and shout the victory.

4

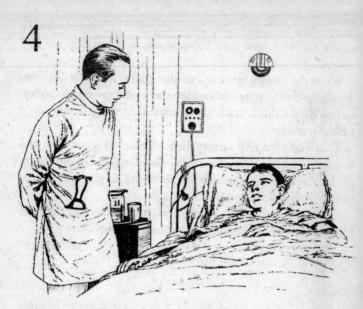

The Father, the Son, and the Holy Spirit

WE HAVE ALREADY LEARNED that there is only one God. Now we must put on our thinking caps and think very hard because I am going to tell you something that you will not understand. But don't feel bad, because no one else has been able to understand it either! And yet it is one of the very most important truths in the Bible.

This is what is so important: our Father in heaven is, of course, God; but did you know that Jesus is God, too, and that the Holy Spirit is God? All three of them are God. And yet there are not three Gods but only one God.

You will probably want to ask me how that can be true.

How can three persons be God, if there is only one God? Could it be that Jesus is just another name for God and is not a different Person? No, the Father, and Jesus and the Holy Spirit are not just three different names for God. They have different work to do. Jesus and the Father made the world and stars and everything else, and Jesus is God. Jesus said, "I and my Father are one."

And when Jesus went from the earth back to heaven to be with God the Father, He sent us the Holy Spirit, who is also God, to be with us.

But there is only one God. Sometimes people have tried to picture or describe how three different persons can be one God by thinking of a three-leaf clover that has three leaves and yet is just one clover. Other people have tried to help us by telling us to think about water. Sometimes water is wet like it is when we drink it, sometimes it is hard when it gets cold and becomes ice, and sometimes it is steam, and yet it is all water, even though it is three things. Or perhaps we could try to imagine three people all having the same mind. These illustrations may help us, but we can never really understand these things until we are with Jesus. But we know they are true because Jesus tells us so in the Bible.

It is so important to know about these things because some people have thought that Jesus was not really God. But if Jesus is not God, then He could not have been our Saviour. Only God can help us; Jesus helps us because He is God.

Do not worry if you do not understand all about these things. When we get to heaven, then we will know, and until then we can obey God and love Him even though we do not understand all about Him.

A man in India once kept asking a missionary to explain about the Trinity—for that is the word we use to mean that there is only one God and that the Father and Jesus and the Holy Spirit are God. The missionary tried to explain this to the man. But the man kept asking more questions about it, so the missionary told him a story. "Once upon a time in a certain country everyone was getting sick. So the king sent medicine to a doctor to give to the people to make them well. One of the sick men had never seen the king, and asked the doctor so many questions about him that the doctor had to spend all his time answering the questions and didn't have time to give the medicine to the people and many of them died.

"When the doctor went back to see the king, the king asked whether he had given the medicine to the people. 'No,' said the doctor, 'I had to explain about where I got the medicine and didn't have time to use it.' "

It is important to know about the Trinity, but our work is to tell people that Jesus died to save them, and not to try to explain to them about the Trinity. We have good medicine for their souls, and we need to use it.

SOMETHING TO READ FROM THE BIBLE: Mark 1:9-11; John 16:7-15

QUESTIONS:

1. How many gods are there?
2. Our one God is three different Persons. Do you know Their names?
3. Can you use the illustration of water to explain about these things?
4. Why did the doctor do the wrong thing in trying to answer all the questions?

A PRAYER:

O God our heavenly Father, You are too great for us to understand, but we thank You that we can understand the love of God.

Help us to grow in Your love and help us to honor the Father.
In Jesus' name. Amen.

> Great is Thy faithfulness!
> Great is Thy faithfulness!
> Morning by morning new mercies I see;
> All I have needed Thy hand hath provided—
> Great is Thy faithfulness,
> Lord, unto me!

5

If We Cannot See God, How Can We Know He Is Alive?

WHO CAN SEE the wind? Neither you nor I! But we don't need to see the wind to know that it is there. We know it is because we can feel it against our faces and see the trees and grass moving when the wind blows. But we cannot see the wind.

We cannot see God either. But we can know He lives by the things He does. Some people say, "If I could see God, then I could believe that there is a God. But I can't see Him, so I won't believe in Him."

But that isn't fair. Those people believe the wind is real when they can't see it, because of what it does. And they can know that God is there because of what He does.

Can you think of some things God does that make us know He is alive?

Well, for one thing, we can see the stars and the sun and moon. Did these just get in the sky by themselves? No, Someone put them there. When we see a house, we don't think it just grew there by itself. We know someone built it. And when we look up at the stars we know they didn't just happen to be there either. Someone put them there. God did.

Do you know why we cannot see God? It is because God doesn't want us to see Him yet. God is so great and so wonderful and so bright that if we saw Him, it would kill us. Some day, if we obey God, He will take us to heaven when we die, and then we can see God as He is. Then it will not hurt us to see Him, but will make us very happy.

Even though we cannot see God we can love Him very much. The Bible tells us about God. It tells us how much He loves us and how good He is. We do not need to see God to love Him.

A mother had been talking to her little girl about loving God. The little girl said, "Mother, I cannot see God and how can I love Him unless I do?"

A few days later the little girl received a package in the mail from a friend she had never seen. In the package was a present. The little girl opened the package very carefully and there inside she found a beautiful picture book. She looked at the book for a long time and then ran over to her mother and said, "Oh, Mother, I love this book and I love the lady who sent it to me!"

"But you have never seen her," said the little girl's mother.

"No," said the little girl, "but I love her because she sent me this present."

That is the way we can love God even though we have not

seen Him. He has given us so many wonderful things such as our homes and our fathers and mothers that we can thank Him and love Him, even though we have not seen Him yet.

SOMETHING TO READ FROM THE BIBLE: Genesis 1:14-28

QUESTIONS:

1. Can you see the wind? How do you know it is there?
2. Can you see God? How do you know He lives?
3. What are some things God does to make us know He is alive?
4. Do you know why we cannot see God yet?
5. When will we see Him?

A PRAYER:

O almighty God, we thank You that the heavens declare Your glory, and that the sun and the moon and the stars, which You have made, show us how great You are. We thank You, too, for the Lord Jesus who has shown us Your great love. In Jesus' name. Amen.

A HYMN TO SING:

"The Light of the World Is Jesus"

Come to the Light, 'tis shining for thee;
Sweetly the Light has dawned upon me;
Once I was blind, but now I can see;
The Light of the world is Jesus.

6

Why God Made Us

WHAT IS THE MAIN REASON why God made us and let us live here in our homes?

Was it so we could be happy? No. God wants us to be happy, but that isn't why He made us.

Was it so we could be kind to other people? No, that is also important, but it isn't why He made us.

Why was it then?

God made us to glorify Him and to enjoy Him. That means that God wants us to thank Him for being so good to us. He wants us to worship Him by understanding how wonderful He is, and how kind Jesus was to come and be punished for our sins, instead of our having to be punished by God. Since God is so great and so good, He wants us to tell Him how happy we are that He has let us be His children. He wants us to be so glad that we will always be wanting to help other people as a way of making God glad.

Do you see now why it was that God made us? It was so that we would love God and always do what He wants us to do, just because we do love Him so much.

Do you love God? That is why He made you.

Once there was a man named Billy Bray who loved God very much. He liked to sing about God because he knew God liked to hear him. Some people thought he sang too much because he couldn't sing as sweetly as other people could, but Billy Bray told them a bird like a crow could only say "Caw Caw," and couldn't sing as nicely as a canary, but God made the crow as well as the canary and He liked to hear them both; and, said Billy Bray, "My heavenly Father likes to hear me sing, too, even though I don't sing much better than the crow."

If we love God, He wants us to tell Him about it.

A HYMN TO SING:

> Praise God from whom all blessings flow
> Praise Him, all creatures here below;
> Praise Him above, ye heavenly host,
> Praise Father, Son, and Holy Ghost.

SOMETHING TO READ FROM THE BIBLE: Psalm 148

QUESTIONS:

1. Did God make us so that we could love Him?
2. Do you know what a traitor is?
3. If God made us for Himself and we serve ourselves instead, what are we?
4. Does God like to hear us sing His praises if we sing like Billy Bray?

A PRAYER:

Our Father, help us to glorify Your great and holy name. Help us to praise You and to live for You always. In Jesus' name. Amen.

ANOTHER HYMN TO SING:

> I love to tell the story,
> 'Twill be my theme in glory
> To tell the old, old story
> Of Jesus and His love.

7

Some Other Things About Our Wonderful God

How MANY THINGS do you know? Did you ever try to count them? You know about cats and dogs, and reading and adding, and many other things. But Mother and Father know much more than you do. Sometimes people go to school all their lives and learn more and more. But even at the end of their lives they do not know very much because there is always so much more to learn. But there is one Person who knows everything. I think you know who that Person is. It is God. There is nothing that God does not know. God made everything and knows everything. He knows what you are thinking now, and knows what you were thinking yesterday, and knows what you are going to think about tomorrow. He knows what happened a million years ago, and He knows what is going to happen a million years from now. He knows whether or not you love Him. We cannot hide anything from God because He is everywhere and knows everything and never forgets anything.

Another very wonderful thing about God is that He can do anything He wants to. He made the world, and He can destroy it if He wants to. There is nothing that is too hard for Him. He can make us well when we are sick; He can send the storms or make them go away. He can forgive us for our sins and take us to heaven.

And God never changes. He is always the same—the same yesterday, today and forever. He does not grow old and weak like people do. Perhaps you have a dear grandmother and grandfather who are no longer as strong as they used to be. People change. Sometimes they are strong, but then they become weak. But God is always strong.

God knows everything; He is so strong that He can do anything He wishes; and He never changes. He is always loving us. What a wonderful God!

A story is told about Dr. Martin Luther, who was one of the great leaders of the Christian church many years ago, of how he once forgot that God is so wonderful. Dr. Luther was worried about many things, because he forgot how great God is, and that God does not change, and that God could take care of things so that he didn't need to worry about them.

One morning when Dr. Luther came downstairs to breakfast, he found that his wife was all dressed in black clothes such as people used to put on when someone had died.

"Oh," said Dr. Luther to his wife, "who has died?"

"Don't you know?" she replied. "God is dead."

"How can you say such a foolish and wicked thing?" he

asked. "How can God die? He will live through all eternity. He never changes. He can never die."

"Then," asked his wife, "why are you so discouraged, if God is still alive?"

"Then I saw," said Dr. Luther, "what a wise woman my wife was. She was trying to make me see that God is truly the same, and that He loves us and will take care of us, and we do not need to be afraid. He is always the same wonderful God."

SOMETHING TO READ FROM THE BIBLE: Psalm 8

QUESTIONS:

1. Name some of the things that God has made.
2. What are some of the things God knows, but people don't know?
3. Will God some day grow old like people do?

A PRAYER:

Our eternal Father in heaven, we thank You that there is no one else like You. We thank You that you are all powerful, that You never change and that You always love us. Help us, we pray, to make You happy by the way we live for You. In Jesus' name we ask it. Amen.

A HYMN TO SING:

O worship the King, all glorious above,
O gratefully sing His power and His love;
Our Shield and Defender, the Ancient of Days,
Pavilioned in splendor, and girded with praise.

8

Who Are the Angels?

A LONG, LONG, LONG TIME AGO, long before God made Adam and Eve, even before He made the sun and the moon and the stars, God made some beings, or people without bodies to live with Him in heaven.

They are called angels.

We cannot see or talk with them, but they see us and some of them are right here in the room with us now, listening and watching. The angels are very kind and helpful, and God has asked at least one angel to be a special helper to each one of us and to keep many things from happening to us that would hurt us.

Of course, it is good for us to be hurt sometimes because that makes us want God more. God has not said that we are never to have anything unhappy happen to us, but God has asked the angels to help us in many ways.

I wonder what the angels think when they are watching us. They probably are so happy that they hardly know what to do because the Lord Jesus died for us and we can go to heaven.

How surprised and pleased they must have been when they saw the Lord Jesus decide to leave His wonderful glory in heaven and come down to the earth and be born as a little baby! You probably remember how the great choir of angels came to the shepherds on the hillside that first Christmas night, praising God and telling about the Lord Jesus being born in Bethlehem.

But, oh, how sad the angels must be when they see us quarreling and acting as if we did not know how much God loves us and how much He has done for us! The angels are watching you and me, and we should live in a way to make them happy and glad.

Some angels are greater than others. The Bible tells us the names of some. There is Gabriel who is a special messenger of God. He was the angel whom the Lord sent to Daniel when Daniel prayed many days to God. There was an angel too that closed the mouths of the lions when Daniel was thrown into the lions' den, but we do not know whether this was Gabriel. Gabriel also appeared to Zacharias to tell him that he was going to have a son, John the Baptist. And God sent Gabriel to the Virgin Mary to tell her that the Lord Jesus was going to be born and that she was going to be His mother.

Then there is Michael, one of the greatest of the angels, or possibly the greatest of all. He sometimes has to fight with Satan.

We do not know the special names of other angels, but we know there are different ones who have different work to do.

The angels are made by God, just as we are, and so we are not to worship the angels, but only to worship God. The angels cannot do anything they like, as God can, and they do not know everything, as God does, and they can only be one place at a time, instead of everywhere at once, as God is.

We sometimes think and even sing that it would be wonderful to be an angel, but it is really much more wonderful to be just who we are—God's own children. This is far better than just being a helper as the angels are. It is much better to be a child of God than just His servant. So we should not want to be angels, but we should be oh, so glad that God has saved us and is going to take us to heaven to be with Him forever.

Most of the time we cannot see the angels, but sometimes people who are dying see them even though other people who are in the room can't see them at all. The people who have seen them tell us how beautiful they are.

Would you like to hear a true story about some angels that one young man saw? He was a helper to a man named Elisha who was one of the prophets God had sent to give His message to the people of Israel.

Some people didn't like Elisha and wanted to hurt him, because he was a man of God and told the people to stop being bad. The king decided to have Elisha brought to him so that he could hurt him. The king sent an army to catch Elisha. The soldiers came to the city where he was staying. Early the next morning the young man helping Elisha got up and went outside and saw a great army of many, many soldiers all around the city, who had come to get Elisha. The man ran to Elisha and said, "Oh, Elisha, what shall we do now? There are soldiers everywhere and they have come to catch you."

Elisha said, "Don't be afraid! There are angels all around to take care of us."

Then Elisha prayed to God and said, "Lord, please open this man's eyes so that he can see the angels you have sent to take care of us." Suddenly the man saw that there were horses and chariots of fire all around Elisha and himself. When the soldiers came, Elisha asked God to make all of them blind for a while so that they couldn't catch him, and that is what God did. God sent His angels to take care of Elisha.

SOMETHING TO READ FROM THE BIBLE: Acts 12:5-17

QUESTIONS:

1. Who are the angels?
2. Can you give the names of two of God's greatest angels?
3. Will you ever be an angel?
4. Is it better to be an angel or a Christian?

A PRAYER:

Our Father, who has made the angels to be Your servants, we thank You that they take care of us. We thank You that we are Your sons and not just angels. Help us to act as Your children. In Jesus' name. Amen.

A HYMN TO SING:

Holy, holy is what the angels sing,
And I expect to help them
   make the courts of heaven ring;
But when I sing redemption's story,
   they will fold their wings,
For angels never felt the joys
   that our salvation brings.

9

Who Is Satan?

SATAN IS A PERSON we cannot see. He tries to do us harm. At first he was good. He was one of God's greatest angels. He was God's important helper and happily did whatever God wanted him to do. How glad he must have been to be able to talk with God and to see God's glory and power!

Then came a sad, sad day, such a sad day that we can hardly think how unhappy it was. On that day Satan decided that he would disobey God. He decided he no longer wanted to love God. We do not know why Satan decided such a terrible thing; we do not know where such as idea came from into his mind, but that is what happened. He became jealous of God and said that he wanted to be like God. Then he became

37

God's greatest enemy, seeking to hurt God instead of trying to help. It was very foolish of Satan to think that anyone could hurt God, because God has all power and can do anything. Someday God will punish Satan so terribly that we do not like to think about it. God made the lake of fire which we call hell in which to punish Satan forever and ever.

Millions of good angels decided to become bad and to go with Satan. These wicked angels are called demons, and they are all around us, but they cannot hurt us if we love the Lord Jesus Christ, because God has sent His good angels to take care of us, and the Lord Jesus Himself is living in us. The demons are very, very much afraid of the Lord Jesus because they know that someday He is going to send them into eternal fire forever.

Satan is always trying to cause us to do bad things. He talks to us and says, "Oh, it is all right to steal that cookie, because it is a good cookie and no one will miss it if you eat it. Go ahead and steal it." But remember, if we obey Satan we sin.

Satan is very strong, and we must be very careful to always love the Lord Jesus so that Satan will not have a chance to hurt us and to get us to do wrong things. We must be very careful not to laugh about Satan and his demons because even Michael, the archangel, did not act like that when Satan was trying to keep him from doing God's work. Instead, Michael said, "The Lord rebuke you, Satan." The Lord can always take care of Satan. We cannot, and we must not try.

We must be careful, too, to stay away from places where the demons or wicked angels come and talk to people. There are some men and women called Spiritists who know how to get the demons to speak in a voice that people can hear, and the demons pretend to those people who listen that they are their friends who have died. The Bible tells us to have nothing to do with that kind of people, because Satan always lies and so do his demons.

One day a little boy, who was not a Christian, and did not know about the Lord Jesus, was standing in front of a fire. Then a demon, one of Satan's bad spirits, entered the little boy's body and made the little boy want to jump into the fire. He jumped in and was badly burned. His father came and pulled him out and saved him.

For a long time after that, the demon would make the little boy do things like jumping into the fire that would hurt him very badly. One day the father took the little boy to the Lord Jesus and asked Jesus to send away the demon from inside his little boy. Jesus told the demon to go and never to come back; and, of course, the demon had to obey Jesus because Jesus is God. Then the little boy was all well again.

SOMETHING TO READ FROM THE BIBLE: Isaiah 14:12-17

QUESTIONS:

1. Why did God need to make hell?
2. Who is Satan and what was he once like?
3. Who is stronger, Satan or God?
4. What does Satan want you to do?

A PRAYER:

Almighty God, Creator of heaven and earth, we thank You that the powers of Satan cannot hurt us when we stay close to our Lord Jesus Christ. We thank You that Satan and his wicked demons are so much afraid of our Saviour. Help us to stay close to Jesus and to love Him always. In Jesus' name we ask it. Amen.

Faith is the victory!
Faith is the victory!
Oh, glorious victory,
That overcomes the world.

10

How God Made Adam and Eve

WE DO NOT KNOW when it was that God decided to make the stars and the world and the animals and the people and everything else, but the time finally came when He did.

Do you know what tools God used to make all these things? When you and I make things, we need paper and crayons and scissors or perhaps a saw and boards and hammer and nails. But it was not so when God made the world. He didn't need any tools at all. He made everything out of nothing. There was nothing, and then He spoke and told the world to begin and there was the world. He told the sun to begin shining, and it did. He made cows and horses and fish and grasshoppers and birds and trees and grass and flowers. It was a very good world God made; it did not have thistles and briers in it; the animals did not try to hurt each other or to eat each other up, as they do today.

And finally, when the beautiful earth was all ready, God made Adam who was the first man. God took some dust from the ground and used it to make a body for Adam; and then God made the body come alive.

How do you think Adam felt when he first knew that he was alive? It must have been a strange and wonderful feeling! He saw the beautiful world that God had made for him. God talked with him and he and God were good friends. Perhaps Adam asked God where he had come from, and God told him.

Then one day the Lord God decided to make another person; but instead of making another man, He made a woman. And she was named Eve. God did not make Eve out of the ground; instead He put Adam to sleep, and while Adam was sleeping, God took one of his ribs and used it to make the woman. Then He gave the woman to Adam to be his helper. Eve must have been surprised and pleased to be alive, and she and Adam and God must have had very happy times together. Adam and Eve had no wrong thoughts of any kind. God made them so that they did not have any naughtiness in them at all. They were pure and sweet and clean and strong. God loved them and they loved God very much.

At school some of our books and some of our teachers may not know about how the first man became alive, and may not know that God made Adam and Eve. People who don't know very much about God sometimes think that a long, long time ago—millions of years ago when nothing was alive—a little piece of earth, too tiny to see, came alive. It had children a little larger than it was, and a little different; and these children had other children that were still larger, and after millions and millions of years a little speck of earth became a man. I don't think God made Adam that way, because the Bible seems to say that God made him suddenly. How great God is! He can do anything in a moment. How easy it was for Him to take some dust of the earth and make Adam from it in a moment of time.

One day a man wanted to teach his little boy about God. It was springtime so he took a shovel and went out into his garden. He used his shovel to make some ground very soft and ready to put in seeds. Then he smoothed it all off and drew in the soft earth the letters J-O-H-N which spelled the little boy's name. Then he put seeds in the lines he had marked so that when the seeds grew, the little plants would spell out J-O-H-N.

Several days later the little boy came running to his father in great excitement and said, "Father, my name has grown in the garden." The little boy took his father by the hand and led him out to the garden and said, "See, Father, it is my name."

"Yes," said the father, "perhaps it just happened to grow there by itself."

"Oh, no," said the little boy, "somebody must have planted the seeds to make the letters."

"Couldn't the letters just grow there by themselves?" asked the father.

"Oh, no," said the little boy, "somebody must have planted them."

"Then," said the father, "look at your hands and your feet; your hands are made just right for you to use to work and to play. Why don't you have your feet where your hands are and your hands where your feet are? Did they just happen to grow in the right place, the way they are?"

"No," said the little boy. "Somebody must have made my hands for me and put them in the right place."

Then the father told the little boy about God, who made all things, and the little boy never forgot that lesson.

SOMETHING TO READ FROM THE BIBLE: Genesis 2:7-25

QUESTIONS:

1. What was Adam made from?
2. What was Eve made from?
3. What was the earth made from?
4. How long did it take God to make Adam?

A PRAYER:

O God, our heavenly Father, we thank You that You are so great, and that by a single word the earth could be made. We thank You for Your great power and for Your great love. In Jesus' name. Amen.

A SONG TO SING:

> The birds upon the treetops sing their song,
> The angels chant the chorus all day long;
> The flowers in the garden blend their hue,
> So why shouldn't I, why shouldn't you
> Praise Him too?

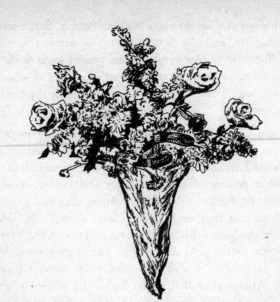

How Sin Came into the World

DO YOU REMEMBER who Satan is? Do you remember how he disobeyed God and could no longer be God's helper, but must be punished forever? Satan was not pleased when God made Adam and Eve because they loved God and were happy. He decided to try to get Adam and Eve to disobey God. If they did, then they would not be happy either. God would need to punish them and send them away forever.

So Satan went down to the earth and talked to Eve. Satan told Eve that God would not do what He said.

God had told Adam and Eve not to eat the fruit of one of the trees that was in the middle of the garden. When Satan came to talk to Eve, Satan told her that the fruit would be good for her and would make her very happy. Satan told Eve a terrible lie, and she believed it. She decided to disobey God. She went to that very tree and picked some of the fruit God told her not to eat, and ate it and gave some to Adam, and he ate it, too. That was one of the saddest days the world has ever known.

Do you know what happened? At the very moment they ate the fruit, Adam and Eve began to die. They lived for many years after that, but they were not happy years, and all the time they were getting older and weaker and sadder. God sent them out of the beautiful garden where they had lived, and told them that they could never, never return. Outside the garden there were thistles and thorns and briers and brambles and weeds, so that poor Adam could hardly grow enough food to eat; also the lions and bears and tigers wanted to attack Adam. Always after that Adam had to be careful where he went. These things happened because Adam and Eve disobeyed God; and their children disobeyed too, and so did their children's children; and all of us have been bad ever since.

Just think what it would be like now if no one in the whole world was ever bad. There would be no war, no robbers, no murderers. Everyone would be kind and sweet and helpful to everyone else. There would be no terrible punishment after death for those who had sinned.

Terrible things came into the world because of that one sad day when Adam and Eve turned away from God and decided to do what He said they must never do.

Adam and Eve thought that disobeying God would not hurt them very much. That is what Satan wanted them to think.

He tries to get us to think that what God tells us isn't important. Satan tells us that nice things will happen if we don't do what God says; but instead, terrible things happen to us, and then it is too late.

There is the story about a wicked man who wanted to scare and hurt another man. He took some pretty flowers that the other man especially liked, and made a lovely bouquet. Then he got a small snake that was poisonous and whose bite would hurt badly and put the snake in the middle of the bouquet. He gave the beautiful flowers to the other man. The man was very pleased and thanked him. But when he bent to smell the flowers, the snake bit him on the face.

That is the way Satan gives us things. They look beautiful but they bring us only harm and sorrow. When Satan tells us to do something wrong, we should remember the story about the snake hiding among the pretty flowers.

SOMETHING TO READ FROM THE BIBLE: Genesis 3:1-19

QUESTIONS:

1. Who is Satan?
2. Does he love God?
3. Does he want you to love God?
4. What did Satan tell Eve?
5. What happened to Adam and Eve after they had sinned?

A PRAYER:

O, our heavenly Father, how sorry we are for our sins! We are sorry that we sometimes listen to Satan instead of listening to You. Help us to stay close to You and not be fooled by Satan. In Jesus' name we ask it. Amen.

Love lifted me! Love lifted me!
When nothing else could help,
Love lifted me.
Love lifted me! Love lifted me!
When nothing else could help,
Love lifted me.

12

God Plans for a Saviour

WE HAVE ALREADY READ about that dark, sad day when Adam and Eve sinned. God's friends became His enemies. Adam's and Eve's hearts were evil, always bad. Satan had come in and was making everything go wrong.

But God was not willing that Adam and Eve should have such wicked hearts; He was not willing that they should live forever and ever away from God in the darkness of hell. God loved Adam and Eve very much even though He had to punish them. God loves you very much, too, even though you have hurt Him so much by your sins.

God had a plan so that He would not need to punish you. His plan was that God would punish Himself for your sins instead of punishing you. God said, "I will suffer so that the boys and girls and their fathers and mothers will not need to. I will send Jesus, my only Son, down to the earth and there I will let Him die for their sins."

And that is why Jesus was born as a baby in Bethlehem. That is why He grew up without doing a single, tiny thing that was wrong. Not once. But God punished Him. Did God punish Jesus because of His own sins? Oh, no, Jesus had no sins. God punished Jesus instead of you, instead of me. He punished Jesus for your sins. Wicked men took Jesus and nailed Him to the cross, and He died for you. God hurt Him so much that we cannot even think how much. Jesus wanted to be punished for you. How kind He is!

One day a man had stolen some money, and a policeman took him to jail. The man was brought to the judge to decide how long he must stay in jail. The judge was very much surprised when he saw who it was that had stolen the money. It was a friend of his. The judge had to do the right thing and could not let the man go home just because he was a friend, so the judge said, "You must give back the money to the man you stole it from and you must go to jail for thirty days."

"But I don't have any money," said the man. "I spent the money that I stole."

"All right, then," said the judge, "I will pay the money for you," and the judge paid back the money to the man whose money was stolen.

"Now," said the judge, "I will go to jail for you and stay there for thirty days and you can go home and take care of your family."

So the judge went to jail and stayed there for thirty days, and the man who stole the money went home.

That is a little bit the way it was about God and us. God

said that we must suffer for our sins. And then He suffered in our place when Jesus died for us.

I think we can never ever thank God enough for being so kind to us. Do you?

SOMETHING TO READ FROM THE BIBLE: Luke 22:39-46; Luke 23:27-38

QUESTIONS:

1. How much does God love you?
2. How much do you love God?
3. How can you show Him your love?

A PRAYER:

Our heavenly Father, we know that the Lord Jesus loved us enough to die for us. Please help us to love Him and to give Him our lives. Our lives belong to You, and we need help to use them for Your work. We ask this in Jesus' name. Amen.

A HYMN TO SING:

"The Old Rugged Cross"

So I'll cherish the old rugged cross,
Till my trophies at last I lay down;
I will cling to the old rugged cross,
And exchange it some day for a crown.

13

Some of God's Friends

AFTER ADAM AND EVE were sent away from the beautiful garden where God had made them, they had to work very hard to get enough to eat. But that wasn't the worst thing that happened when they disobeyed God. Even sadder was what happened when they had children, because their children were bad, too, just like their father and mother had been, and were always sinning. The children of those children were perhaps even worse and so it went on until the world was full of sinning people. They were so bad that God finally told a man, whose name was Noah, to build a big boat called an ark. God said that He was going to send a rainstorm, and it would rain so much that all of the ground would be covered with water. It would rain until all the houses were covered, and until all the trees and hills were covered too. The people would be drowned except Noah and his wife and his sons and their wives.

God did send the great flood and all of the people drowned.

Noah believed and obeyed God. Probably his family did, too, because Noah would have brought them up to love God. The boys would not have wanted to marry girls who did not love the Lord.

At last the flood was ended, the water gone, and all the sinful people were drowned. Only the people who trusted God were left. Wouldn't you think that from that time on there would be only happiness in the world and no more sin and sadness? But that isn't what happened. Do you know why? It was because there was still sin in Noah and in his family, even while they were trying to love and obey God. That's the way it is in our hearts, too; even after we are Christians there is sin that is always ready to rise up and make us do wrong things unless we let Jesus rule our hearts completely.

Well, before very long there were children born to Noah's sons. But the children were bad, and even Noah's sons were sinners and so was Noah. And so when the world became full of people once more, they were all sinners, and it was just as it had been before the flood.

We cannot get away from our sins except by the blood of the Lord Jesus Christ who died to take our sins away, and help us to live the kind of lives that God wants us to live.

Three thousand years ago in the land of Egypt a king died and was buried in a great pyramid. Many things were placed beside him, things that he had especially liked when he was alive. Because he liked food, there was a jar of corn near his head.

When this grave was discovered a few years ago, some of

the corn was taken out and planted in a garden. Do you think that corn three thousand years old could grow? Yes, it did, and it sent up its green stalks and had some more corn.

Sin in our heart is something like that corn. No matter how old we become, the sin in our hearts is always ready to grow whenever it has the chance. Don't give it a chance to grow! Let Jesus be the One to take care of your heart, and He won't let sins grow there.

SOMETHING TO READ FROM THE BIBLE: Genesis 7

QUESTIONS:

1. Did Adam and Eve do something bad?
2. Were the children of Adam and Eve bad too?
3. Why did God send the flood?
4. How good were Noah and his children after the flood?
5. Why can't you and I be good all the time?
6. What shall we do about it?

A PRAYER:

Our Father in heaven, we recognize that our hearts are very bad and full of sin. We thank You for forgiving us and we thank You for helping us keep from sinning. We thank You in Jesus' name. Amen.

A HYMN TO SING:

Jesus never fails,
Jesus never fails;
Heaven and earth may pass away,
But Jesus never fails.

14

My Good Shepherd

Do you know what the Lord Jesus is doing away up there in heaven? One of the things I like to think about most is that He is watching over us and telling all the angels that we are His children and that our sins have been forgiven. When Satan comes to God and tells God what bad things we have done, Jesus says, "Yes, but I died for those sins." And then He asks the Holy Spirit to make us sorry that we have done those bad things, and He helps us to tell God that we are sorry that we have done them. He is our Good Shepherd and He helps us to be good children of God.

Jesus loves other people, too. He helps us to tell them about God. He makes His children able to do different kinds of work so that many different kinds of people can hear that

Jesus died for them. That is why our fathers do not all work at the same place. The Lord Jesus has given each daddy a different kind of work so that he will be with different people who need to know about Jesus. God loves all His children and He loves these other people too, even if they don't love Him.

A story is told about a father and mother who did not have very much money, but they had six children. One day a rich man came to the mother and father and said, "I will give you some money if you will let me have one of your children to be my own, because I do not have any children."

The mother and father looked at each other and tried to think which one of their children they might be able to let the man have. They thought about their oldest boy, Tim, but they shook their heads, "Oh, no," they thought, "we can't let him have Tim." Then they thought about Sue, and again they shook their heads. They thought about each of the other children but each time they shook their heads and said, "No, not that one; no, not that one." Finally, they had come to the last one and said the same thing.

The rich man said, "I will give you a hundred dollars."

The parents said, "No."

"I will give you a thousand dollars."

The mother and father said, "No."

"I will give you ten thousand dollars," said the rich man.

What would you have said? I think you would have said just what that mother and father said. They said "No, we will not let you have any of our children."

Jesus loves us even more than that mother and father loved their children. He will not let anyone have us. He is always thinking about us and loving us while He is up there in heaven.

SOMETHING TO READ FROM THE BIBLE: Romans 8:35-39

QUESTIONS:

1. When Satan says that we have sinned, what does Jesus say?
2. How much does Jesus love us?
3. Will He give us away?

A PRAYER:

Our Father, we thank You that You love us so much that no one can take us away from You. Help us to love You, too, and to try to please You with all that we do. We come in Jesus' name. Amen.

A HYMN TO SING:

Jesus loves me! this I know,
For the Bible tells me so;
Little ones to Him belong;
They are weak, but He is strong.
Yes, Jesus loves me,
Yes, Jesus loves me,
Yes, Jesus loves me—
The Bible tells me so.

15

The Most Important Thing a Child Can Do

DID YOU EVER TRY to think what is the best thing that anyone can ever do? We can think of many things. Perhaps we would think first of all about being kind to each other, or about obeying Mother and Daddy. These are very, very important. We might think about how important it is to eat enough, or to get enough sleep. These things are important, but there is something else that is the most important of all.

Shall I tell you what it is?

The most important thing is to obey God, and do just what He wants us to. When you obey God, it makes Him very happy and He gives you many lovely things.

He is saving some of His best presents for you. He will give them to you after a while. He is saving them for you until the time when you go up to be with Him in heaven. How wonderful it is going to be then, if you obey God now!

He likes to give lovely things to boys and girls who obey Him. Can you think of some of these things? I will tell you one of them and then you can think of others. One thing He gives obedient children is happiness. If they obey Him, they are happy, and if they don't obey Him but do naughty things instead, then they are unhappy.

What happens if you don't obey God? Does that make any difference? Well, what happens when you don't obey your mother or father? They must punish you. God must punish you, too, if you disobey Him.

A Sunday school teacher was talking to the children in her class about obeying God, and she told the children that God's will is to be done on earth just as it is done in heaven. She asked, "Children, how do you think that God's will is done in heaven? How do you think that the angels and the happy spirits do the will of God?"

The first child replied, "They do it right away, as soon as they know what God wants them to do."

The second child said, "They do it just as well as they possibly can, because they are doing it for God."

The third child said, "They always do just what God wants them to and don't try to think of other things to do instead."

None of the other children in the class could think of anything else until after a while one little girl put up her hand and said, "Teacher, I think they do it without asking any questions."

Isn't that a good way to do God's will?

QUESTIONS:

1. What is the most important thing a child can do?
2. What are some of the things God gives us when we obey?
3. Can you tell one of the ways the children in the story said was the way to obey God?

A PRAYER:

Dear Lord Jesus, help us to obey You in all things. May the Holy Spirit help us to want to do Your will. This we ask in Jesus' name. Amen.

A HYMN TO SING:

Trust and obey,
For there's no other way
To be happy in Jesus,
But to trust and obey.

16

What Happens When We Ask Jesus to Be Our Saviour?

LONG, LONG AGO—long before you were born—millions of years ago—God knew that you were going to be born, and He loved you. Throughout all of those long, long years He was thinking about you and waiting for the time when you would be born.

But God was sad all that time, too, because He knew that almost as soon as you were born, you would do wrong things that He did not want you to do. He knew that you would be born with sin in your heart. He knew that He would need to punish you because of your sins. God did not want to punish you for being bad, and He found a way to save you. He decided to take the punishment on Himself instead of punishing you. So it was decided that Jesus, God's Son, would leave His wonderful home in heaven and come to earth and be punished for your sins and mine.

And that is just what happened. God did send Jesus, and Jesus died for you, and now you may ask Jesus to be your Saviour.

Are boys and girls or their fathers and mothers saved from God's great anger if they do not want Jesus to be their Saviour? No, they must want Jesus, and they must love Him and serve Him.

Perhaps you do not know how to ask Jesus to be your Saviour. It is not a hard thing to do. Jesus already knows when we want to be saved. He wants us to come and talk to Him about it. We can talk to Jesus in prayer, and we could say something like this: "Dear Lord Jesus, I have done many wrong things, and I have made God very displeased because of the things I have done. God does not want to punish me by sending me to hell and so He punished You, Lord Jesus, instead of me. He punished You for my sins. I thank You, Lord Jesus, for being so very kind as to suffer and die for me. I could not help myself but You saved me."

You do not need to use these same words because God knows what you mean, and the words you use are not important. But sometimes saying the words helps us realize what Jesus has done for us.

A father used to take his little son into his arms and talk with him about Jesus. The little boy never grew tired of that sweet story. One day while sitting in his father's lap, his father said to him, "Would my little boy like to go to heaven?"

"Yes, Daddy, of course I would," he answered.

"But," said the father, "how can you go to heaven? Your

little heart has sin in it. How can you expect to go where God is?"

"But all are sinners, Daddy," the little fellow answered.

"That is true," replied the father, "and yet God has said that only the pure in heart shall see Him. How then can my little boy expect to go there?"

The little boy's face grew very sad, and he began to cry. And then suddenly a smile broke through his tears and he said, "But, Daddy, Jesus can save me."

Yes, Jesus was glad to save that little boy, and He wants to save you, too. Have you asked Jesus to save you? He wants you to talk to Him about it.

SOMETHING TO READ FROM THE BIBLE: John 3:1-18

QUESTIONS:

1. Who was punished for your sins?
2. Do we have to pay any money to Jesus to save us?
3. If we pay Him a lot of money will He save us?
4. Why did Jesus die on the cross?

A PRAYER:

Dear Lord Jesus, we know that we cannot ever pay enough to get to heaven, but we thank You that You have freely given us eternal life so that we can be forever in heaven with You. In Jesus' name. Amen.

A HYMN TO SING:

"Let Jesus Come into Your Heart"

Just now, your doubtings give o'er;
Just now, reject Him no more;
Just now, throw open the door;
Let Jesus come into your heart.

17

Why Did Jesus Save Me?

THE STORY IS TOLD about a man who had a pet pig. The man always kept the pig smoothly brushed, with a ribbon around its neck. The pig would follow the man wherever he went. What a very strange pet!

One day the man was taking a trip across the ocean in a big boat and was walking around the boat with his pig behind him. Somehow, the pig managed to crawl through the railing and fall into the ocean. The man who owned the pig rushed up to the captain and said, "Oh, my pig, my pig, my pig has fallen overboard! Stop the ship! My pig will drown."

The captain of the great ship laughed at the man. "We cannot stop this ship for a pig," he said.

"If it were a man who fell overboard would you stop the ship?" asked the man who owned the pig.

"Yes, of course," said the captain. Then the man who owned the pig ran over to the edge of the ship and jumped into the ocean and the great ship had to be stopped and turned around and both the man and the pig were brought back into the ship.

Wasn't that a rather foolish thing to do, to risk one's life for a pig?

But do you remember that Jesus gave His life for us and we are worse than pigs—we are sinners? Jesus went down into the ocean of sin where we were and lifted us out and gave us to God, who is the Captain of the ship. God gladly took us and made us His children. Now we are saved sinners and have been changed into sons and daughters of God. Now all the angels as well as Satan and his evil friends can see how wonderful God's love is! It is so wonderful that it was able to take us even though we are sinners, worse than pigs, and give us new hearts that love the Lord Jesus. All of the angels in heaven are praising God for what He has done for you. They are glad because you love Jesus.

Sometimes when people grow flowers, they have a contest to see who can grow the prettiest ones. Do you know that if you belong to the Lord Jesus you are now a beautiful flower in His garden? You are not like a pig. Now Jesus can bring the angels into His garden and show you to them as an example of how kind and great and good God is! Of course, we are not talking about a real garden and real flowers, but we are talking about how much Jesus loves you and how He has changed your heart.

It is too bad that we are not yet all that God wants us to be. If we look at one another we can tell that we still do many wrong things, and our lives are not very pretty. But God likes to think of us as we will be after we die, and when He looks down and sees us, He is able to see that we are forgiven and that we will be beautiful flowers in His garden some day. Of course, I do not mean that you are going to be turned into a flower. Thinking of pigs and beautiful flowers may help us to realize how much God has done for us and is going to do.

SOMETHING TO READ FROM THE BIBLE: Luke 15:3-7, 11-24

QUESTIONS:
1. Can a pig change himself into a lamb?
2. Can sinners change themselves into children of God?
3. Who can change us into children of God?
4. Tell how to become a child of God.

A PRAYER:

Thank You, Lord Jesus, for dying for me. Amen.

A HYMN TO SING:

"Grace Greater Than Our Sins"

Grace, grace, God's grace,
Grace that will pardon and cleanse within;
Grace, grace, God's grace;
Grace that is greater than all our sin.

18

If I Try to Be Good
Will Jesus Save Me?

Do YOU KNOW that we can never be good enough to be saved? Some people think, "If I try to be real good and do whatever Mother and Daddy tell me to, and do what the teacher says, and am kind to the other children and never quarrel or fight or become angry and don't steal anything or hurt anybody, then I will be such a good boy or girl that God will take me to heaven."

But this is not true. That is not the way we get to heaven. The trouble is that no matter how good we try to be, we keep doing and saying and thinking things that are not good. Probably every single day—no matter how hard we try—we have at

least one cross word or thought. That means that our hearts
are still naughty.

And even if we could keep from doing one single naughty
thing all the rest of our lives, what about the naughty things
that we did last year or yesterday or even today? How shall we
get rid of those naughty things?

How many sins does it take before God needs to punish us?
Does it take one hundred sins? No, it takes only *one,* and all of
us have sinned not only once, but many, many times.

And besides, when Adam and Eve sinned there in the Garden of Eden by eating the fruit of the tree that God told them
not to, it did something to them so that their children were
born with naughty hearts. That is why even a very small child
often does not want to do what his mother tells him to, and
can become very angry and naughty.

Since we are born with naughty hearts and have done so
many bad things, God can't let us come to heaven just because we are trying to be good. No, God always punishes sin,
and He must punish your sins even though you promise to try
to be good from now on.

But He punished Jesus instead of punishing you. Jesus
died for your sins and took your punishment. How much
Jesus must have loved you to be willing to die in your place!

Jack had stolen a bicycle and then had left it out in the
street. A car had run over it and wrecked it. It was Billy's
bicycle, and Billy knew that Jack had stolen it. Billy said,
"Jack, you must buy me a new bicycle."

"Oh, no," said Jack, "I am sorry that I stole your bicycle
and that it was wrecked, but I will not steal another bicycle
from you. If I try to be good, I will not need to pay for the
bicycle."

Was Jack right? Is it enough to be sorry and to try to be good?

SOMETHING TO READ FROM THE BIBLE: Romans 3:10-18, 23

QUESTIONS:
1. Have you ever done a wrong thing? What was it?
2. How many wrong things must we do to keep us out of heaven?
3. How can you get to heaven?

A PRAYER:

Our Father in heaven, we have sinned and done many wrong things but we thank You that Jesus died for our sins and has gone to prepare a place for us in heaven. In Jesus' name. Amen.

A HYMN TO SING:

> At the cross, at the cross where I first saw the light,
> And the burden of my heart rolled away,
> It was there by faith I received my sight,
> And now I am happy all the day!

19

A Child of the King

SOMETIMES WE SAY that a Christian is a child of God. What does this mean? Does it mean that we don't have our father and mother anymore? Oh, no, it doesn't mean that at all. God has given us our fathers and mothers to take care of us and love us. But we have Someone else now who loves us even more and can take care of us even better. That Someone is God.

When we love His Son Jesus, He adopts us into His family and we become His children as well as the children of our mothers and fathers. Isn't that a wonderful thing?

Have you ever wondered why God lets us be His children? Why would He want children who have sin in their hearts and who are so selfish and unkind? We can't understand why

He is so kind, but the Bible tells us that God is not ashamed to call us His children. He never wants to get rid of us or to make us go away. He loves us even when we are bad. He doesn't have favorites whom He wants near Him, and others whom He doesn't like very well. He loves you with all His love; always, even when you have been bad, He still loves you just as much. Even when He must punish you, still He is loving you with all His love, because you are His very own child if you love Jesus as your Saviour.

When God becomes your Father, then Jesus becomes your elder Brother. How strange and wonderful to have as a Brother the One who made us and who made the world! But Jesus is God's Son, and we are God's children, so Jesus has become our loving big Brother. The Bible tells us that He is not ashamed to call us brothers.

He is not ashamed of us because He died to make us good, and to make us His little brothers and sisters. He died to make us part of His family, the family of God; and so now Jesus shares with us all the good things that God has given to Him. He gives us eternal life. He will take us to heaven and give us wonderful things there. He will take away all of our sins so that we will finally be the kind of children of God that we ought to be.

Once there was a great king who was very rich. He had many servants and lived in a beautiful castle made of gold. One day when the king was walking along a street with some of his servants, he saw a little beggar boy who was very poor and had big holes in his clothes. The king found out that the little boy didn't have a mother or father so the king took him home to live in the palace, and the little boy became the king's son. The king loved his new son and gave him many wonderful presents. When the little boy was old enough, he helped the great king rule part of his kingdom.

You and I are like the little boy because we were taken into God's family, and He gives us many wonderful gifts, and someday He will ask us to help Him rule.

SOMETHING TO READ FROM THE BIBLE: Romans 8:14-17

QUESTIONS:

1. Does God want us to be His children because we are so good?
2. Can anyone become one of God's children? How?
3. Does God still love us when we are bad?
4. How does God punish us? Does He still love us when He punishes us?
5. If God is our Father then Jesus, His Son, is our elder B.....

A PRAYER:

Dear Father, how glad we are that You have been willing to let us be children of Yours and brothers of our Lord Jesus Christ. We thank You for being so kind to us. We come to You, O God, in Jesus' name. Amen.

A HYMN TO SING:

I'm a child of the King,
A child of the King:
With Jesus my Saviour,
I'm a child of the King.

20

Where Was Jesus Before He Was Born?

AT CHRISTMASTIME we sing about Jesus being born in the manger, and we read about how the angels and the shepherds and wise men were so glad because He was born.

But did you know that Jesus was alive and was with His Father in heaven for millions of years before He was born that night in Bethlehem? He had always been in heaven with God because He is God. Up there in heaven millions of angels bowed down before Him, sang beautiful songs to Him about His brightness and His goodness.

One day while He was up there in heaven, He made the world; and, on another day, He made Adam and Eve. But

Adam and Eve disobeyed God and became sinners. They had to be punished, but Jesus did not want them to be punished. He does not want you to be punished. He said, "I will go and die, and be punished for their sin."

The day finally came when the Lord Jesus left heaven and the millions of angels who loved Him, and He came way down to this world and was born. But He was not really like other babies because He is God. How much Jesus loved us to be willing to become a little baby, so that He could grow up and die for our sins!

An old man over ninety years of age was asked by his pastor one day, "My dear aged friend, do you love Jesus?"

The man's deeply wrinkled face lit up with a smile, because he had loved Jesus for sixty-seven years. He grasped the minister's hands with both of his, and said, "Oh, I could tell you something better than that."

The minister asked him, "What is that?"

"Oh, sir," said the old man, "it is that *He loves me*. He loved me when He was with God in heaven before He came to be born as a baby in Bethlehem. He loves me now, and He will love me forever, after I have died and gone up to heaven to be with Him."

SOMETHING TO READ FROM THE BIBLE: John 14:1-12

QUESTIONS:

1. Do you know how many years ago Jesus was born in Bethlehem on that first Christmas morning? If not, ask Mother or Daddy.
2. Where was Jesus before He was born?
3. Why did Jesus decide to leave heaven and come down and be born?

4. Does Jesus love you?
5. Do you love Jesus?

A PRAYER:

Dear Lord Jesus, we thank You for being willing to come from heaven and live here on the earth for a few years. We thank You for coming to die for us. Help us to live for You. In Your name. Amen.

A SONG TO SING:

Thank you, Lord, for saving my soul,
Thank you, Lord, for making me whole,
Thank you, Lord, for giving to me
Thy great salvation so full and free.

21

How the Baby Jesus Was Different from Every Other Baby

CHRISTMAS is a happy time. It is a time when we remember how God gave us a wonderful gift and that gift was Jesus.

We love to read about the time when Jesus was born in Bethlehem, and how the angel talked to the shepherds on the hills and told them about Jesus; and how they came and worshiped. You remember, too, how the wise men came bringing their gifts to Jesus.

Did you know that there was a strange and wonderful thing about the way Jesus was born? It is that Mary was His mother, but her husband, whose name was Joseph, was not Jesus' father. Jesus did not have any man for His father like you or I do. God was Jesus' Father.

Why is it important that God is Jesus' Father? What difference would it make if Joseph were His father? Well, if Joseph were Jesus' father, then His father would not be God; and if God were not Jesus' Father, then Jesus would not have been able to heal the sick people or make dead people alive again. But worst of all, if Joseph were Jesus' father, Jesus would be just like you and me with a heart that has badness in it. And if Jesus had a bad heart, He could not have died for us. He would need to die for His own sins, not ours. But Jesus didn't die for His own sins. He didn't have any, because God is His Father. You see now why it is so important for us to know that Joseph was not His father.

When we talk about this strange and wonderful fact that Jesus had a mother but no man for His father, we say that Jesus was born of a virgin. No other baby ever born was born of a virgin because every other baby had to have a father; but Jesus did not need a human father. God was already His Father.

Once a man was watching some ants run about on the ground. He followed them to where they lived and found a great anthill with thousands of little ants inside it. And the man thought to himself, "If I wanted to talk to those ants, how would I do it? I could shout at them, but they would not hear or understand me. I could write a letter to them, but they would not read it." Finally he thought, "If only I could become an ant myself then I could speak to them and they could understand me."

Then the man thought, "That is the way God did it, too. He decided not only to look down from heaven at us, but to become one of us so that He could tell us about His love. That

77

is why Jesus came and was born as a little baby and grew up to tell us of God's love and to show God's love by dying for us."

SOMETHING TO READ FROM THE BIBLE: Matthew 1:18-25

QUESTIONS:

1. Who was Jesus' mother?
2. Who was Jesus' Father?
3. Who was Joseph?
4. Would it have made any difference about our sins if Joseph had been Jesus' father?

A PRAYER:

O God our Father, how wonderful it is that Jesus is Your Son! We thank You that He had no sin and that He died for us and for our sins. We want to be included among those for whom He died. We thank You that You are willing to receive us. In Jesus' name. Amen.

A HYMN TO SING:

> Silent night! holy night!
> All is calm, all is bright
> 'Round yon virgin mother and Child,
> Holy Infant so tender and mild,
> Sleep in heavenly peace,
> Sleep in heavenly peace.

22

The Miracles of Jesus

PROBABLY YOU REMEMBER some of the wonderful things Jesus did while He was here on earth. Do you remember about the time Jesus and His disciples were in a boat going across the Sea of Galilee, and a great storm came up? Perhaps you can tell the story about how the disciples were so afraid, but Jesus just kept on sleeping. The disciples rushed over to Jesus and woke Him up. They said, "Master, don't You care that the boat is sinking and we are all going to drown? Why don't You help us?" Jesus was sorry that they were afraid, for He knew that they didn't trust Him to take care of them. He told the wind and the waves to be quiet, and immediately the storm was gone.

And there are many other true stories. Do you remember

about the time when a friend of Jesus died, whose name was Lazarus? His friends buried him, and Lazarus had been dead for four long days and nights when Jesus came. Jesus went to the place where Lazarus' body was buried and told Lazarus to become alive again. And Lazarus came back to life.

And do you remember another time when Jesus fed thousands of people with just four or five small loaves of bread and some little fishes? As He broke the bread and the fish into pieces, there was always more to break and give to the people.

Another time, when a little girl was sick, Jesus told her to be well; and instantly she was well without any medicines or any doctors.

Jesus did many, many wonderful things like that. It is a good thing for us to think about these wonderful deeds of Jesus, because they are miracles. A miracle is something that God does that people can't do. The doctor can't make a little girl well instantly; and no one can bring dead people back to life, except God.

Because Jesus is God, we would expect that He would want to do some of these wonderful miracles so that people would know that He is different from other people.

After Jesus went back to heaven, God gave this power to do wonderful things to Peter and to Paul and to others of His disciples. Then Peter was able to fix up a man whose foot was crooked; Peter told the foot to get well, and all at once the foot was all right. Another time Peter had been put in jail because he was telling people about Jesus. God sent an angel to break open the locks of the doors and to take Peter's chains off his hands and feet. This was a very wonderful miracle.

Sometimes magicians, who are men who perform magic tricks, can do things that seem very wonderful. But magicians only do tricks and make us think that something really happens when it doesn't happen at all. One of their favorite tricks is to show us the inside of a hat that is empty and then pretty soon pull a rabbit out of the hat. This is to make us think that the magician made the rabbit and that he can make things out of nothing. But this, of course, is not true. He put the rabbit into the hat when we were not looking.

Some people who do not love the Lord Jesus have said that perhaps the miracles Jesus did were tricks, too, like the magic man does. But no magic man could ever make a dead man come back to life, or do the other things that Jesus did. No, Jesus is not a magic man, He is God; and so, of course, He can give people life if He wants to.

Do miracles still happen today? Yes, sometimes they do. Sometimes when we pray for people who are very sick, when the doctors cannot help them anymore, God makes them well. Usually He lets the doctors do this, but sometimes He does it without using their knowledge and their medicines.

Whenever we pray, we are expecting God to perform a miracle, we are asking Him to do something that we cannot do ourselves. We are asking Him to step in and do the things for us, because they are too hard for us to do.

Here is a true story about a miracle. One day a missionary lady was riding along a road in faraway China. Suddenly some robbers came and took all of her money, and they took away her glasses too. She needed her glasses very much and could not read very well without them. There was no eye doctor for hundreds of miles who could give her new glasses. She asked God to help her, and on the way back to her house she remembered that she had another pair of glasses put away in a drawer at home. When she got home, she found this pair of glasses and thanked the Lord that she had them. Then she put the glasses on. But they didn't work; instead, everything she read looked blurry. So she took off the glasses very sadly, and what do you think she noticed? She noticed that she could read perfectly well without the glasses! God had cured her eyes so that she didn't need the glasses anymore. God had answered her prayer. She had prayed for glasses, but, instead, God had fixed her eyes so that she didn't need glasses. This is a true story, and a wonderful example of miracles that can still happen today.

Does God always do a miracle whenever we ask Him to? No, sometimes He doesn't want us to have the thing we pray for. We must be careful to ask Him to give us only the things He thinks we ought to have, and not ask Him for just anything we think we might like. And then we must be glad and trust Him.

SOMETHING TO READ FROM THE BIBLE: Mark 6:32-44

QUESTIONS:
1. What is a miracle?
2. What was one of the miracles Jesus did?
3. What is a magician? Can he do miracles?
4. Can you think of any miracle that Jesus did for you after you had prayed about something?

A PRAYER:

Dear Lord Jesus, we thank You for the wonderful miracles of long ago as when the blind man was made to see. We thank You, too, for wanting us to pray to You and that You are willing to do wonderful things for us today. Help us to pray and to trust You. In Jesus' name we ask it. Amen.

> All hail the power of Jesus' name!
> Let angels prostrate fall;
> Bring forth the royal diadem,
> And crown Him Lord of all;
> Bring forth the royal diadem,
> And crown Him Lord of all!

23

The Death of Jesus Christ

NOW WE MUST TALK about one of the strangest and most terrible and yet wonderful things that has ever happened. Do you remember (chapter 12) how Adam and Eve ate the fruit God told them not to eat? That was the first time sin was in their hearts, and at that very moment their bodies were changed so that they began to grow old and die. And all the world around them became different: there were thorns now, and thistles, and briers that suddenly began to grow up; and animals, like the lions and tigers, began to want to kill the other animals like the sheep, and wanted to eat up Adam and Eve, too. All of these strange and unhappy things happened because Adam and Eve had sinned.

But far worse than anything else, God had to say that Adam

and Eve deserved to live in hell, forever and ever away from God. Oh, what a terrible, terrible thing to ever happen. How we wish that Adam and Eve had obeyed God and never, never sinned.

But never forget that God loved Adam and Eve, even as He loves you; and you have sinned just as much as Adam and Eve, and deserve just as much punishment. Because God loved you He decided that He would punish Jesus in your place.

You or I could not be punished for someone else's sins, because we have so many sins of our own that we need to be punished for. But Jesus, the Son of God, never sinned. He was the only One ever born into this world who could die for someone else's sin. He died for your sins.

Do you know how Jesus died? Some men who did not like Him, took Him and nailed Him to a cross made out of wood; and there He died. It hurt the Lord Jesus very, very much, because there were nails put through His hands and His feet. Jesus suffered more than just His bodily pain. We cannot begin to understand the ways that Jesus suffered, but we know that for the first time God turned His face away from His Son, and the Lord Jesus was in darkness away from God. Just think! Jesus, who didn't need ever to suffer or die, wanted to suffer and die for you, and He did.

And now you can have your sins forgiven! So can each one who wants to be saved. If you tell God that you accept Jesus who died in your place, God is ready to forgive you.

About one hundred years ago, when men in the army did not do what their officers told them to, sometimes they were whipped with long, hard pieces of leather that would cut into the skin of their backs and make their backs bleed. Of course, this hurt very much. One day the soldiers living in a certain tent stole some money from some soldiers living in the next tent.

But the men would not tell which of them stole the money. The officers told them they would all be punished with whips unless they would tell which of them had done it.

Then, a boy named Willie, who was really too young to be a soldier—but they let him anyway—stepped forward to the officer and said: "Sir, punish me so that the other men in the tent will not have to be punished. I did not take the money, but I want to be punished for the men who did take it."

The leader was very sorry, because Willie had not stolen the money and should not be punished; and, besides, Willie was not very strong, and he was afraid that if he punished him it might make him sick. But the officer finally decided to whip Willie.

They tied Willie to a tree and took his shirt off, and then the officer began to whip him. The big whip cut deeply into Willie's back, but he did not scream. Again the whip came down, and there was another deep cut in his back.

A third time it came down, and then one of the men, the one who had really stolen the money, jumped forward.

"Stop, stop!" he said, "I stole the money. Do not whip Willie anymore. Whip me instead."

But Willie said, "No. He has already whipped me, and he cannot whip you now. I have taken your whipping for you."

And so they let the man who had stolen the money go free and did not whip him, because they had whipped Willie instead.

That night Willie died, because he had been hurt so much. Perhaps this helps you just a little bit to see how it was that the Lord Jesus Christ—the One who made the heaven and the earth and you—came down to earth and was punished so that you could go free.

Have you thanked Jesus for dying for you?

SOMETHING TO READ FROM THE BIBLE: Isaiah 53:1-12

QUESTIONS:

1. When was it that God made the thorns and thistles and briers?
2. Before Adam and Eve sinned, what were the animals like; did they try to hurt each other? How did the cats and the mice get along?
3. What happened to Adam's and Eve's hearts when they disobeyed God? If there were no sin in the world, would there be any quarrels? Why or why not?
4. Could we be punished by God for someone else's sin if we wanted to help him out? Why not?

A PRAYER:

O God, our heavenly Father, we know that even little children who disobey God need the Lord Jesus to save them. We thank You so much that He died for us. Help us, dear Father, to love and trust Him, and to obey Him always. In Jesus' name we ask it. Amen.

A SONG TO SING:

> For God so loved the world,
> He gave His only Son,
> To die on Calvary's tree,
> From sin to set me free;
> Some day He's coming back,
> What glory that will be!
> Wonderful His love to me.

24

Jesus Becomes Alive Again

PETER AND JAMES AND JOHN and the other disciples were terribly sad when Jesus died on the cross. They thought that He was going to be their King because He had done so many miracles, and had told them so many things about God. They were very much surprised that God would let Jesus die. They probably wondered if He was really God's Son, after all; or whether instead He was just a kind of wonderful friend who had died.

For three days, the disciples went around not knowing what to do without Jesus. Then, one day, on a Sunday morning when some of the disciples went to Jesus' grave, they were surprised to see that the grave was empty, and that Jesus' body was not there. They thought someone had come and stolen

His body away, or perhaps moved it somewhere else to bury it. While they were wondering about this, angels came and told them that Jesus had become alive again, that God had made Him alive and soon He would come and talk to them. The disciples could hardly believe this; but not very long afterward, while they were talking together, suddenly Jesus was there with them. He looked just like He had before, but now He had a new body and could go right through walls, and could be in a room with them without having come in at the door at all. Suddenly He would be there and just as suddenly He would be gone.

God has promised to make His children alive again after they die. Can He do it? Oh, yes, we know He can because He made Jesus live again, so now it doesn't make very much difference if we die, because we will become alive again. God has said so!

Some people say, "How do you know that Jesus really did come out of the grave?" One of the ways to know that Jesus was dead and then became alive is to notice what happened to His disciples. They had been very sad when Jesus died, but three days later they became so happy they hardly knew what to do with themselves, because they had seen Jesus again. Most of them were finally killed because they kept saying Jesus was alive. And, of course, they wouldn't have said it so much, when they knew they would be killed for saying it, unless they really believed it—unless they had really seen Jesus alive again.

Three days after Jesus had died, two of His friends were walking along a road, and they were very, very sad. They talked to each other about how Jesus had died when they thought that He was going to keep on living forever and would become a great King. As they were talking together, suddenly a third Man came up to them and walked along with them. He asked them why they were so sad, and they told Him that it was because Jesus had died.

Then the third Man said, "Why, don't you know that the Bible says that Jesus would die? Don't be surprised that He died, because it was told us that He would." Then this third Man began to tell them all that the Old Testament said about Christ dying for our sins. He made them see that if Jesus hadn't died, then their sins couldn't be forgiven.

The two men asked Him to come to their home and talk with them some more, and He did. They had just sat down at the supper table when all of a sudden something happened: they saw that the third Man was Jesus Himself. Jesus was the One who had told them why He had to die. They were too much surprised to know what to do, and just then Jesus suddenly disappeared.

How happy they were that they had seen Jesus! How good it was that Jesus had come and explained these things to them, so that they need not be sorry any more!

They quickly got up from the table and went to their friends and told them that Jesus was alive, because they had seen Him.

SOMETHING TO READ FROM THE BIBLE: John 20:1-18

QUESTIONS:

1. Why were the disciples surprised when they went to Jesus' grave?
2. What had happened to Jesus?
3. After Jesus became alive again what could His body do that yours and mine cannot?
4. Can you tell the story about Jesus and His two friends walking along the road?

A PRAYER:

Our Father in heaven, we thank You because Jesus was made alive again. We thank You that because He lives, we shall live also. Help us to think a great deal and often about Your love and power. In Jesus' name. Amen.

A HYMN TO SING:

> Only believe, only believe;
> All things are possible,
> Only believe;
> Only believe, only believe;
> All things are possible,
> Only believe.

25

Jesus Goes Back to His Father in Heaven

HAVE YOU EVER BEEN away from Mother and Daddy for a day or two? Perhaps it was when you were visiting with some friends or with Grandmother. Do you remember how glad you were to get home again? And even if you have never been away from home, you can imagine how good it is to come back to Mother and Daddy.

When Jesus left His Father in heaven and came to the world to live, He was gone from home for thirty-three long years. Can you think how He must have longed to go back to His Father and home with the glorious angels? Finally, the thirty-three years were ended, and it was time for Him to go back to heaven.

He took His disciples out to a little hill, and while He was talking to them, He began to rise into the sky over their heads. A cloud moved to where He was, and He went into the cloud, and they didn't see Him anymore.

We don't know where He went except that we know it was to heaven to be with His Father. We don't know where heaven is. Perhaps it is millions and millions of miles away. But probably it was only a moment after He went into the clouds that He was in heaven, at home again.

How wonderful it must have been when Jesus got there! Millions of angels were there waiting for Him, singing songs of glory and joy and happiness because their Lord Jesus was home again. They bowed down before Him in wonder that He would have left the glories of heaven to go down to the earth to save you and me. Now He was back again, and they watched as God, the almighty Father, welcomed Jesus, His Son, back to the glorious throne upon which they both could now sit forever.

Is Jesus still there in heaven? Yes, He is still there. Do you know what He is doing? I will tell you. He is getting our homes ready for us. He is waiting for us to come and live with Him. That will make Him very happy!

And He is doing something else. He is praying for you. And whenever you sin, He reminds God that you belong to Him, that He died for your sins.

Some day, perhaps very soon, Jesus will once more leave heaven and come down to earth to lead all His children up to heaven, and they will be with Him forever after that.

A boy said to his mother, "Mother, I don't quite understand why it was such a great thing for Jesus to die for us. If I could save a dozen men by dying for them, I think I would. And I would certainly would want to if there were a million of them."

"You cannot understand," said his mother, "because you cannot begin to imagine what Jesus had to go through to save us. But, my son, would you die for a dozen grasshoppers?" That started the boy thinking. After a few days he came to his mother with his doubts all gone.

"I don't know about the grasshoppers, Mother," he said, "but if it were a million mosquitoes I think I would let them die!"

In thinking of ourselves and God, we are not nearly as important as we often think we are; and yet God sent His Son to die for us, and He now lives forever praying for us and will come and take us to be in heaven with Him forever.

SOMETHING TO READ FROM THE BIBLE: Acts 1:9-14

QUESTIONS:
1. How long was Jesus away from His Father in heaven?
2. Tell about how He left the disciples to go back to His Father.
3. If you had been an angel in heaven when Jesus came back, how do you think you would have felt?
4. Where is Jesus now?
5. What is He doing?

A PRAYER:
Lord Jesus, there in heaven watching over us, hear us now as we pray to You. We thank You that You have loved us so much and that some day we will go to live in heaven forever. While we are waiting for that time, help us to live our lives here in ways that will always be pleasing to You. We pray in Jesus' name. Amen.

What a Friend we have in Jesus,
All our sins and griefs to bear!
What a privilege to carry
Everything to God in prayer!

26

Jesus Is Coming Again

SOME DAY, we do not know when—it may even be today—our Lord Jesus is going to come back from heaven and take us with Him into heaven. What a day that will be! At last we will see our Lord Jesus. He has not told us when this will happen because He wants us to be ready for Him to come at any time. He wants us to be expecting Him and doing right things. If He told us just what day and what year He was coming, then perhaps we might not remember as well to live good lives every day. We might wait until the day He was going to come before we would try to live like we should, and then it would be too late because we would not be in practice.

So Jesus has not told us when He is going to come.

And we don't know how He is going to come. God has told

us, though, all we need to know about it. The Bible tells us enough to let us understand one important thing. The important thing is that He is coming back to take us to be with Him forever. The Bible tells us, too, that there is going to be a new heaven and a new earth. This world is going to be burned up, and God is going to make everything new and fresh and lovely, and there will be no sadness or sin or sorrow.

Two boys were talking about Jesus' coming back again. One of them said, "I wonder what it will be like on the highways when the cars keep going after the people are taken out of them. There will be some terrible smashups."

"I wonder what it will be like on the trains," thought the other boy.

"And think of the airplanes," said the first boy.

And then the second boy said a very wise thing, "I don't think that we should think about what is going to happen. I think we should think about how we should live for Jesus now."

And that boy was right.

Would you like to see Jesus? Would you like to be able to bow down and worship and thank the One who gave His life for you?

Maybe you can, even today, because even today He might come back and take you to be with Him forever.

SOMETHING TO READ FROM THE BIBLE: I Thessalonians 4:13-18;
    I Thessalonians 5:1-6

QUESTIONS:
1. When is Jesus going to come back?
2. Why does it help us to do good things if we think He might come today?

We thank You, Lord Jesus, that You are coming again. Help us to think of You every day and to be ready for Your coming. In Jesus' name. Amen.

A SONG TO SING:

Every day with Jesus
Is sweeter than the day before,
Every day with Jesus
I love Him more and more;
Jesus saves and keeps me,
And He's the One I'm waiting for;
Every day with Jesus
Is sweeter than the day before.

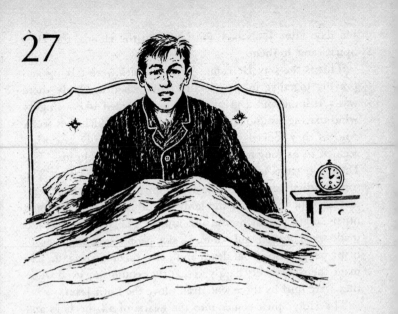

27

The Holy Spirit

DO YOU KNOW who the Holy Spirit is? Do you remember that
there are three Persons who are God, and yet there is only one
God? Well, the Holy Spirit is one of those three Persons. We
call Him God the Holy Spirit; the other two Persons are God
the Father and God the Son.

The Holy Spirit has always been alive. When Jesus made
the world, the Holy Spirit was there, too, and each Person had
His part in the work.

When Jesus was talking to His disciples one day, just before He died for us, He told them that He was going back to
His home in heaven to be with God the Father; and He told
them that He would send them the Holy Spirit. Sure enough,

ten days after Jesus had gone up into the clouds, the Holy Spirit came to them.

This is the way He came: The disciples were talking and praying together in an upstairs room when suddenly there was a rushing and a great noise that sounded like a mighty wind roaring around and filling the house in which they were. And as they looked at each other, they suddenly saw what seemed to be tongues of fire sitting on their foreheads. The Holy Spirit was being sent to them by the Lord Jesus. The tongues disappeared, but the Holy Spirit stayed within them, and each of these men suddenly was able to speak in some other language that he did not know. The Holy Spirit also made some of them able to make sick people well and even to bring people back from death and make them alive again. He made them very, very happy so that they could sing even when they were hurt by those who didn't love the Lord Jesus.

The Holy Spirit comes into the hearts of all the boys and girls who love the Lord Jesus and helps them live for Him. He is in your heart if you are a Christian. All heavenly thoughts and desires are from Him. He helps you to trust and obey. He helps you to be pure and lovely and honest. Because of Him you can have love and joy and peace and happiness in your heart. Your body is His home, and He is the One who will bring your body back to life again after you have died.

The Holy Spirit is not only in your heart, if you are a Christian, but He is also in heaven praying for you. You don't know how best to tell God about many things, but the Holy Spirit takes your poor, weak prayers and makes them right and powerful. Because the Holy Spirit is God, He can pray in such a way that God will hear and answer. The Bible tells us that the Holy Spirit prays for you with sighs and groanings too deep for words. This means that He cries out to God for you and for the things that you are praying about. Is it not wonderful that you have this help of God Himself in your praying?

The Holy Spirit not only helps you but He helps people who are not Christians by making them want to love God. He helps them understand what Jesus has done for them.

And it is the Holy Spirit who helps you understand the Bible when you read it; if you have trouble understanding, just pray and ask the Holy Spirit to help you.

The way the Holy Spirit sometimes does this work is shown in the following story:

A man who did not love God at all, but hated Him, was invited to come to a meeting to hear the gospel preached. The man laughed and said that he would never come. Several people who loved the Lord Jesus decided that they would pray for the man. They met that night and prayed for a long, long time. In fact, they prayed all night for this man to be saved from his sins.

The man they were praying for went to bed that night as usual, but about two o'clock in the morning he suddenly woke up. He began to think about all of the wrong things he had done and he began to think about God's judgment and the lost eternity that was before him. He began to tremble as he lay in his bed. Then he thought of what someone had once told him about the Lord Jesus dying for him. He leaped out of bed and got down on his knees beside his bed and asked God to forgive him for Jesus' sake. He cried out to God for a long time but finally realized that God had heard him and forgiven him. Then he was so happy that he could hardly wait for morning to tell the friend about it, who had invited him to the meeting the night before. His friend was very much surprised when he heard that people had been praying all night for him. The Holy Spirit had wakened the man and made him see what a great sinner he was.

SOMETHING TO READ FROM THE BIBLE: John 16:7-15

QUESTIONS:

1. Who is the Holy Spirit?
2. Where is He?
3. What are some of the things He does?
4. What does the word "Holy" mean?
5. What can stop Him from helping us the way He would like to?

A PRAYER:

Dear Lord Jesus, we thank You for sending the Holy Spirit to help us in so many ways. Help us to live clean lives so that the Holy Spirit can do whatever He likes in our hearts. In Jesus' name. Amen.

A HYMN TO SING:

Blessed quietness, holy quietness,
What assurance in my soul!
On the stormy sea He speaks peace to me,
How the billows cease to roll!

28

May Christians
Do Wrong Things?

WE HAVE ALREADY LEARNED that we can never be good enough to get to heaven. Only Jesus by His death and resurrection can save us. Does this mean that it doesn't make any difference whether or not we are good? After we become Christians by asking Jesus to become our Saviour, can we just keep on being naughty and expect Jesus will save us anyway?

One of the wonderful things that happens when Jesus comes into our hearts is that He helps us to be good. Why is it, then, that sometimes we still want to do naughty things?

It is Satan who whispers to us to do wrong things. Satan is very strong. He is stronger than even the strongest of the angels, and he knows how to trick us and make us want to be sneaky and bad. When we get to heaven, Jesus will give us new hearts that Satan cannot get into at all, and we will never, never want to do bad things again.

But now, while we are still here on the earth, we still have hearts that can sin. When Jesus comes into our hearts, He will help us to keep from sinning if we want Him to.

How wonderful it will be when we finally get those new hearts; then there will never be anything inside us whispering to us to do wrong, or helping to make us angry!

But remember that Jesus is very much stronger and greater than Satan, and Satan is very much afraid of Jesus. When we ask Jesus to help us, Satan hides.

Do you know something that is very strange about this? I will tell you what it is. Even though Jesus has come into our hearts, He does not make Satan leave us unless we ask Jesus to tell Satan to go away, and unless we ask Jesus to take charge of our lives.

A little girl was asked, "Why is it that you don't do such naughty things as you did before Jesus came into your heart? Doesn't Satan bother you anymore?"

"Oh, yes," said the little girl. "He keeps coming around and knocking at the door of my heart, but I ask Jesus to go to the door for me, and when Satan sees Jesus, he runs away."

SOMETHING TO READ FROM THE BIBLE: Romans 6:1-10

QUESTIONS:

1. What does Satan want us to do?
2. Are you stronger than Satan?
3. Who is stronger than Satan?
4. How did the little girl in the story keep Satan from making her want to do wrong things?

Dear Lord Jesus, we thank You that You are God and that You are stronger and greater than anyone else and that You are more powerful than Satan. Help us to ask You to keep our hearts so that they will be strong and pure for You. In Jesus' name. Amen.

A HYMN TO SING:

"True-Hearted, Whole-Hearted"

Peal out the watchword! silence it never!
Song of our spirits, rejoicing and free;
Peal out the watchword! loyal forever,
King of our lives, by Thy grace we will be.

29

Who Is on the Throne in Your Heart?

Do YOU KNOW what a throne is? It is a beautiful place where a king sits and speaks to his people.

What would you think if I told you that there is a throne inside your heart, with someone sitting on it? I hope you are not on that throne. There isn't really a throne, of course, not a real place to sit, but we can pretend that there is. And there is a real Person in our hearts. He is the King and tells Christian boys and girls what they should do. Do you know who that Person is? It is Jesus.

But there are two other people who try to sit on the throne and tell us what to do. One of them is Satan, and the other one is you. Whenever Jesus wants you to do a certain thing and you do something else instead, that means that you and Satan are sitting on the throne in your heart and deciding what to do. It means that you have told Jesus to leave the throne where He ought to be and that you have decided to sit there yourself. Satan laughs when you do that. He knows that when Jesus is not there, he can get you to do all kinds of bad things. Satan likes you to be angry and unkind and to cry when Mother asks you to help. That is easy for Satan to do when Jesus is not on the throne to help you.

Whenever you are sitting on the throne and being the king of your life, then Satan is not afraid to go all around in your heart-house and make everything go wrong. He knows that he is stronger than you are, and he laughs at you because he is really the king and can do anything he wants to.

But if Jesus is sitting on the throne, then Satan doesn't try to make things go wrong. He stays hidden until you decide you want to be on the throne again.

Our Lord Jesus is very kind, gentle, and tender, as well as very strong. He doesn't stay on the throne unless you ask Him to. One of the biggest and most important jobs you have after you become a Christian is to learn how to keep yourself from wanting to sit on that throne. God will help you if you ask Him to. He will ask the Holy Spirit to keep talking to you about it.

Who is king of your life? Who is sitting on the throne of your heart? Are you sitting on it yourself and letting Satan run your life, or are you letting the Lord Jesus sit there?

SOMETHING TO READ FROM THE BIBLE: Romans 6:14-23

QUESTIONS:

1. Who wants to sit on the throne of your heart?
2. When we are sitting on the throne, what does Satan do?
3. When Jesus is sitting on the throne, what does Satan do?

A PRAYER:

Almighty God, our heavenly Father, we need Your help and we ask that the Lord Jesus will sit on the throne in our hearts and keep Satan from making us want to do bad things. We thank You that Jesus is stronger than Satan. We come to You in Jesus' name. Amen.

A HYMN TO SING:

"I am Thine, O Lord"

Draw me nearer, nearer, blessed Lord,
To the cross where Thou hast died;
Draw me nearer, nearer, blessed Lord,
To Thy precious, bleeding side.

30

Keeping the King on His Throne

Do you remember about the throne in your heart? Do you remember who the three kings are who want to rule there? One of them is the Lord Jesus, the real King, and the others are you and Satan. But when you and Satan sit on the throne and do things just to please yourselves, then Satan can do anything he wants to in your heart and make things go wrong. But when the Lord Jesus is on the throne, then Satan hides and you can be happy and helpful. Then the Lord Jesus is pleased by what you do, and so are Mother and Daddy. Everything is all right when Jesus is ruling your heart, and everything goes wrong when you try to do things just to please yourself.

How can you keep from wanting to have the throne? How can you keep the Lord Jesus always on the throne? Isn't it strange that after Jesus has done so very much for us that we sometimes ask Him to leave and let us run our own lives? And yet that is what we often do. So now I will tell you how you can fix things so that you won't want anybody but Jesus on the throne, so that you will want only Him to be King. This is the way: Get to know Jesus better, and then you will love Him more and want Him to rule. Why does that help—just to know Jesus better? Well, when some new child moves into your neighborhood, maybe at first you don't know whether or not you will like him because you don't know him very well. But if he is an agreeable child, the better you know him, the better you will like him and want him to come and play with you.

And in just the same way the more we know Jesus, the more we will love and trust Him and want Him to do whatever He wants to do. The more we know Him the more we want Him to be always on the throne of the heart.

Wouldn't you like to know Jesus better? Do you know one of the best ways to get to know Him better? That is by talking to Him. That is always one of the best ways to get to know people—by talking to them. But we cannot see Jesus, so how can we talk to Him? We can talk to Jesus by praying. We cannot see Him, but He hears us whenever we speak to Him, even though we may not talk out loud and no one else can hear us at all.

Another way to know Jesus better is by listening to Him talk to us. How does He talk to us? He talks to us when we read the Bible. When we read the Bible, we are hearing God talk to us because the Bible is His Word. We cannot always understand what He is saying, but we do not need to understand everything at once. As we keep reading and thinking or having the Bible stories read to us, the Lord Jesus and His Holy Spirit help us to know Jesus better.

A little boy was very cross and unhappy; in fact, he was so cross that his mother had to scold him and finally she had to spank him and send him to his room. He was there for about half an hour; when he came back he was smiling and his face was very happy. His mother was very glad but she couldn't understand why he was so happy. Finally, she asked him.

The little boy said, "I was so cross at everybody because yesterday at Sunday school our teacher asked us if we would be willing to go to some other country and tell the people there about Jesus if God wanted us to be missionaries. I didn't want to and so I said 'No.' And just then when I said 'No' to God, the Lord Jesus came off the throne in my heart.

"But when I was upstairs I began to think how much Jesus loves me, and that He died for me, and I was ashamed that I was on His throne and telling Him whether or not I would be a missionary. So I told the Lord Jesus that if He wanted me to be a missionary, I would, and I gave up the throne and the Lord Jesus is there now, so I am happy."

SOMETHING TO READ FROM THE BIBLE: Romans 12:1-3

QUESTIONS:

1. How many people at one time can sit on the throne in your heart?
2. Why does it help us to know Jesus better?
3. Can you tell why it is something like a new child coming to your neighborhood?
4. What is a good way to know Jesus better?

A PRAYER:

Dear Lord Jesus, we want to know You better, and we are glad that we may come to You and that You love us. Help us to know You better so that we can love You more and trust You more. This we ask in Jesus' name. Amen.

A HYMN TO SING:

> Have Thine own way, Lord!
> Have Thine own way!
> Thou art the potter;
> I am the clay.
> Mould me and make me
> After Thy will,
> While I am waiting,
> Yielded and still.

31

Bearing Fruit

A BOY AND HIS FATHER were walking along the road. The boy noticed a dead branch that had fallen out of a tree.

"Father," he said, "look at that branch. Let's take it home and plant it so that we can see the leaves come out and see the apples grow on it."

"Oh, no," said his father, "the branch is dead. It cannot have leaves on it and it cannot have apples. It is dead."

"Isn't there any way that we can get it to have apples?" asked the boy.

"No," said his father, "it is dead; the only way would be if God would give new life to the dead branch and make it part of the tree again."

Then the father said to his boy, "We were like that dead

branch and Jesus is like a living tree. We couldn't help ourselves at all; then God took us, the dead branch, and made us
alive, and put us into our place in the living Tree. But instead of growing apples and pears, like the real trees do, we
grow such fruit as kindness, love, joy and goodness."

We were like the dead branch, but now Jesus has made us
alive, and we must bear fruit to prove it.

SOMETHING TO READ FROM THE BIBLE: John 15:1-8

QUESTIONS:

1. Can a dead branch become alive again without God?
2. The Bible says that sinners are dead in sin. Why are they
   like dead branches?
3. What did God do to save people who were dead in sin?

A PRAYER:

*Our Father in heaven, we know that because of our sins we
need a Saviour, and we thank You that You have saved us and
given us new life in Christ our Lord; now cause us to bear good
fruit. In Jesus' name we pray. Amen.*

A SONG TO SING:

> This little light of mine,
> Yes! I'm gonna let it shine;
> This little light of mine,
> Yes! I'm gonna let it shine;
> Let it shine, let it shine, let it shine.

114

32

How Can You Tell Whether Someone Loves the Lord Jesus?

HAVE YOU EVER WONDERED whether someone you know loves the Lord Jesus? Do you know that there is a way you can find out without asking? Sometimes a person may say he is a Christian when he isn't at all. But there is one sure way to know. It is a test that Jesus gave us so we could find out how much we love Him. He says we can tell by the things we do. People who say they love Jesus and then try very hard to please Him— we know they love Jesus. But people who say they love Jesus and then don't do what He tells them to, really can't love Him very much.

What are the things Jesus wants us to do to show that we

love Him? The first thing, and it is the most important, is to be kind and loving to other people. We can be kind to our mothers and daddies by helping them and doing quickly whatever they say. This makes Jesus happy when we obey our parents quickly and cheerfully.

Who else can we be kind to? We can be loving and kind to our brothers and sisters, letting them play with our toys and games; we can be nice to other children at school. Probably you can think of many other ways, too.

If you are not kind to other people, the trouble is that you love yourself more than you love Jesus. If you loved Jesus more, then you would want to obey Him even when you didn't feel like it.

Of course, this isn't easy to do. It takes practice. If you take piano lessons or play baseball or some other game, you know how much practice it takes to do it well. Well, we need to practice, too, when it comes to doing things God wants instead of just the things we want. We need to practice being kind to each other. If someone says an unkind thing to us, it is easy to think of something worse to say about him. But we need to practice forgiving instead. I cannot tell you how very important this is. The Bible tells us again and again that loving other people and being kind to them is one of the most important things about being a Christian. That is the way we can tell how much we love Jesus.

Mr. Brown was a very fine Christian man, but one day his horse happened to get loose and got out of the pasture and into the neighbor's cornfield. Mr. Brown's neighbor was very angry and called the police. They caught the horse and made Mr. Brown pay some money before they would give back the horse to him.

116

A day or two afterward Mr. Brown met his neighbor and the neighbor was still very angry. "If I ever catch your horse in my cornfield again," he said, "I'll call the police again."

"Neighbor," said Mr. Brown, "not very long ago I looked out my window in the night and saw your cows in my pasture. I drove them out and shut them in your feed lot where they were supposed to be; and if your cows ever get into my pasture again, I'll do the same thing again."

Mr. Brown was so kind that his neighbor was sorry he had been angry and mean.

What would have happened if Mr. Brown had become angry, too, and said that if the neighbor's cows got into his pasture again, he would call the police? Do you think Mr. Brown's neighbor would have wanted to become a Christian?

How do you think the Lord Jesus would have felt about it?

SOMETHING TO READ FROM THE BIBLE: I John 2:3-14

QUESTIONS:

1. How can you tell how much someone loves the Lord Jesus?
2. Can you think of some ways of being kind to someone?
3. Does a child need to practice many hours to play the piano well?
4. Does a child need to practice being kind?
5. If someone is unkind to you, what is the best way to get even with him?

A PRAYER:

Dear Lord Jesus, You have been so very kind to us in saving us that we ask You to help us also to be kind to others. Help us to show them Your love so that they will become Your children. In Jesus' name. Amen.

117

> Channels only, blessed Master,
> But with all Thy wondrous power
> Flowing through us, Thou canst use us
> Every day and every hour.

33

What If We Sin After We're Saved?

TODAY WE WANT TO TALK to you about what to do if you love the Lord Jesus but find that you still do things that grieve Him.

When Jesus becomes our Saviour and we have our sins taken away, it does not mean that from that moment onward we will have no trouble with Satan. He will still try to get us to do wrong things, and sometimes when we are not being careful to stay close enough to Jesus, Satan can get us to think wrong thoughts.

What can we do about it? The Bible gives us the answer. It says that we must confess our sins, that is, tell Jesus that we are sorry we have sinned; then He will forgive us and we can be happy again. But what if we don't ask Jesus to forgive us? Then Jesus has to punish us. He lets us get into trouble or He keeps something from us that He would like us to have.

But when we finally come to Jesus and tell Him that we have done the wrong thing and thank Him for His forgiveness, right away the storm is over and we feel His love again. It is like times when we have been naughty and Mother and Daddy have had to punish us. They are unhappy and we are unhappy, but when it is all over and everything is made right, then our hearts are full of joy again.

Some people think that we must go to some other person who doesn't know what we have done and tell him about our sins and ask him to forgive us. But this is not what the Bible teaches. No man or woman can forgive sins. Only God can do that. God tells us that we may and must come directly to Him. He wants *us* to come, not to send somebody else to talk to Him about our sins.

One morning when George's father was leaving for work, he said, "George, will you mow part of the lawn today?"

George didn't like to help mow the lawn but he said, "Yes, Father, I will."

When his friend Bill came over, he said, "Bill, I will give you ten cents if you will mow the lawn."

When George's father came home that evening from work, he was well pleased and said, "George, that is a fine job you did. Here is twenty-five cents." George took the twenty-five cents, but he was not very happy. He did not tell his father that he did not mow the lawn. He knew that he was telling a lie to his father by not telling him that Bill had done it. He felt worse and worse; he felt so bad that he didn't want very

120

much supper, and pretty soon he felt so bad he couldn't stand it any longer.

"Daddy," he said, "I didn't mow the lawn and here is the twenty-five cents. Bill mowed it for me."

Then George's father said, "Thank you for telling me, George; I knew it all the time because I met Bill on the way home and he told me about the lawn. Now let's go out and play ball together."

George was glad he had told his father all about it. Then he asked God to forgive him and he felt happy again. George and his father had a fine ball game then, because George's sin was forgiven.

SOMETHING TO READ FROM THE BIBLE: I John 1:8—2:3

QUESTIONS:

1. If a Christian boy or girl does something wrong, what should he do about it?
2. Can our pastor forgive our sins?
3. How does Jesus sometimes punish us?
4. Why does He punish us?

A PRAYER:

Our Father, we are so glad that our sins can be forgiven. Help us to remember to tell You about anything wrong we do, and to confess our sins. In Jesus' name. Amen.

A HYMN TO SING:

Search me, O God, and know my heart today;
Try me, O Saviour, know my thoughts, I pray.
See if there be some wicked way in me,
Cleanse me from every sin, and set me free.

34

Why It Helps Us
to Be Punished

WHAT DOES IT MEAN to be punished? Well, it means that
something you don't like happens to you because you have
been naughty; when Mother or Daddy scold you, that is one
kind of punishment. When they have to spank you, that is
another kind of punishment. Or perhaps you can't have a
dessert that you especially like.

Are Mother and Daddy just being mean when they punish
you? No, not at all. They are obeying God who says that
children must be punished when they do wrong things. God
says in the Bible that even though we don't like being punished, afterward it makes us better boys and girls. God says

that children must obey their parents and that parents must punish their children when they are bad.

Do you see why this is so? When you do something wrong and are punished for it, you remember not to do it again; and it helps you to understand how much you have offended God by being bad.

What happens when boys and girls are not punished for doing wrong things? Such boys and girls don't obey their parents unless they want to; they don't mind their teachers; and they don't care very much about the laws of their country. Not to obey our parents and the laws is a very great sin. Children who are not punished make other people unhappy, because they don't care whether or not they hurt other people. Sometimes a policeman has to take them away. Then their mothers and fathers are very sad, and they wish that they had helped their boy or girl learn how to be good by punishing them whenever necessary.

So you see, it is not just to be mean that your parents sometimes spank you. They are really being kind to you because it helps you to think about other people and their rights, and about what God wants, instead of thinking only about how to have your own way. Being punished keeps you from getting into a great deal of trouble.

But most of all it is very, very important that we learn to obey our parents at all times and to obey our teachers and to obey everyone who has the right to tell us what to do, because if we don't, it is hard for us to learn to obey the Lord Jesus. So when our parents spank us when we do wrong things, they are really helping us to love the Lord Jesus more and helping us to be ready to do whatever the Lord Jesus says. For when we learn to obey Mother and Father, we are also learning to obey God.

So you see, parents who do not punish their children are really being very unkind to them. The next time Daddy or Mother has to spank you, don't be angry, but think afterward about how it helps you remember to do good things instead of bad things. God will be pleased by this.

A man named Mr. Conrad was looking at the garden of a friend. Both Mr. Conrad and his friend had some children. Mr. Conrad always punished his boys and girls whenever that was necessary, but his friend did not want to hurt his children or make them feel bad, so he did not punish them.

The man who didn't punish his children said, "I think it is best just to let children grow as they like. I don't like to stop them from doing things because it might hurt their personalities. I believe in freedom of expression."

"But," said Mr. Conrad, "I see that you do not believe in letting weeds grow in your garden."

"Of course not!" Mr. Conrad's friend exclaimed. "Why does that surprise you?"

"Your garden is perfectly weeded," said Mr. Conrad. "I don't see a single weed here. Why don't you just let the garden grow?"

"Because the weeds would choke out the good plants," said Mr. Conrad's friend. "I have to keep killing the weeds."

"Yes," said Mr. Conrad, "and in the same way, letting the garden of a child's heart grow without keeping back the weeds will soon mean that the weeds crowd out the good plants the Lord has put there."

Yes, our hearts are like flower gardens. Let us be thankful when our parents help us to keep the weeds out.

SOMETHING TO READ FROM THE BIBLE: Ephesians 6:1-9

QUESTIONS:

1. Why does it help us to be punished?
2. What happens when boys and girls are not punished when they do wrong things?
3. Do you think that it will help us to obey God if we learn to obey our parents?

A PRAYER:

Almighty God, our Father in heaven, we know that because You are our Father sometimes it is necessary for You to punish us because we do wrong. Help us to learn from the punishment. Help us also to be obedient to our earthly fathers and mothers, and to honor them. In Jesus' name we ask it. Amen.

A HYMN TO SING:

> Onward, Christian soldiers, marching as to war,
> With the cross of Jesus going on before:
> Christ the royal Master leads against the foe;
> Forward into battle, see, His banners go.
> Onward, Christian soldiers, marching as to war,
> With the cross of Jesus going on before.

35

A Letter from God

SUPPOSE THAT your mother and daddy were missionaries in some faraway land across the ocean. Would they be able to talk with you? No, they would be too far away, you couldn't hear their voices and you couldn't see them. But there would be a way you could find out the things they wanted you to do! They would write you some letters.

Now suppose that God wanted to talk with you. If He came to visit you, you would not be able to stand the brightness all around Him. But there is a way He can talk to you; He sent you a long letter for you to read! His letter is the Bible. It tells many things about God, about His work, and about you and what He wants you to do. Have you been reading His letter?

God did not write the letter with a pencil or fountain pen as you and I might do, nor use a typewriter. Instead, He chose about forty men who loved Him and put it into their minds to write the different books of the Bible. Sometimes the Lord would give them a dream or make them see pictures of things that were going to happen, and then they would write these things down. Probably they did not know that they were helping to write the Bible. They just knew that God had told them to write down what they saw, and that is what they did. But then God saw to it that what they had written was kept, and, finally printed in our Bibles.

Sometimes the men wrote about how much they loved God. King David was one of the men who did this. We call the part of the Bible he wrote the Psalms.

At other times these men wrote about what happened to their friends who sinned and were punished by God. Probably they often didn't realize, while they were writing these things, that God was telling them what to say and keeping them from making mistakes.

Do you know how long it took to write the Bible? It took more than fifteen hundred years! One year God would tell one man to write part of the Bible and maybe a hundred years later God told another man to write some more. And sometimes two men were writing different parts of the Bible at the same time. This went on until the Bible was finished.

Did these men make any mistakes while writing the Bible? No, God kept them from mistakes.

How kind God was to give us this letter so that we could know about heaven and about the Lord Jesus and about His love for us!

But how would you feel if you wrote a letter to someone who didn't read it? I think you would have hurt feelings. And

I think that is the way God feels if you don't read His letter. So it is very important for you to read God's letter or have it read to you so that you may know what it says. You may not understand all of it, but you can understand some now, and more as you grow older.

Susan was watching her mother read the Bible.

"Mother," she said, "why do you read the Bible so much?"

Mother smiled at Susan and said, "Susan, why do you drink so much milk and eat toast so often?"

"I have to, Mother," Susan said, "because I'd get so hungry if I didn't; and if I didn't have any food I'd die."

"That's true," her mother said, "but we have something else besides our body to keep alive. Inside our body is our soul. It needs food, too."

"Oh, now I understand," said Susan; "we must read the Bible every day to find food for our souls just as we eat and drink to keep our bodies alive."

"Yes," said her mother, "and if tomorrow you went without breakfast and again at dinner you couldn't eat, what would I think?"

"You would think I was sick," Susan said.

"I surely would," said Susan's mother; "and it is a sign of our being sick in our souls when we don't read God's Word. Other books can keep our minds alive, but only God's Word can feed our souls."

SOMETHING TO READ FROM THE BIBLE: II Timothy 3:14-17;
II Timothy 4:1-2

QUESTIONS:

1. How can you give someone a message without talking to him?

128

2. What is the way God has chosen to give us His message?
3. How long did it take to write the Bible?
4. If we don't read God's letter will it make any difference?

A PRAYER:

O God, our heavenly Father, we thank You for Your letter to us, the Bible. Help us to do whatever it tells us. May it be a light unto our feet and a lamp unto our path. We ask this in Jesus' name. Amen.

A HYMN TO SING:

"Standing on the Promises"

Standing, standing,
Standing on the promises of God my Saviour;
Standing, standing,
I'm standing on the promises of God.

36

How Do We Know the Bible Is True?

THE BIBLE is the most important book in all the world because it tells us things about God. It tells us that God made the world and the first man and woman. None of us were there to see God do it, so we could never know about it unless God had told us in the Bible.

But some people say that since we did not see God make the world, we cannot know for sure whether He did it or not; they say that we cannot know whether the Bible is telling the truth when it says God created the world, and when it tells us other things about God. How can we help people know the Bible is really true?

I don't think we can make people believe anything if they don't want to. They can always think of reasons why something might not be true. It would be hard to prove that you are reading this book or that it is being read to you! Perhaps you are only dreaming it! Of course, you aren't, but someone could say you are, and it would be hard to prove that you aren't having a dream.

In the same way it is very hard to prove things about God to some people, if they don't want to believe about Him; but we can help them in several ways that I am going to tell you about now.

One of the best ways is for us to know that even though the Bible was written so long ago, it told about things that were going to happen after the Bible was written. And sure enough, the things happened. The Bible told thousands of years ago that the Jewish people would be taken away from their country of Israel and that God would bring them back to live there again. Well, that is what is happening today. That is something we can see and prove, and know that the Bible was right when it said that this was going to happen.

The Bible tells about many kings of various countries who lived long, long ago. People who did not like the Bible used to say that these kings never lived and that the Bible was wrong; but now it has been found that these kings did live after all, and just at times and places where the Bible says they did.

Because the Bible proves true whenever we can test it, we can certainly believe that it is also true about things that only God knows and tells us in the Bible.

One of the best ways of all to know that the Bible is true is because it tells us how to have our sins forgiven and tells us that our lives will be changed by the power of God when we accept the Lord Jesus as our Saviour. And every time someone comes to God and asks God to forgive him his sins for Jesus' sake, and means it, that person's life becomes very different. This is one of the best proofs that the Bible is true.

A man who did not think that the Bible is true happened to find a Bible lying in the road. It made him very angry because he didn't know it was a true book; he tore it up, pulled the pages out, and scattered them along the road.

A robber was hiding in the bushes beside the road, ready to jump out and rob the man who had torn up the Bible. But when he saw the parts of the Bible lying along the road, he decided not to rob the man yet but to see what was making him so angry. After the man had gone by, the robber went down and picked up one of the pages of the Bible, and as he was looking at it he noticed the words, "Believe on the Lord Jesus Christ and you will be saved."

"Oh," he thought, "how wonderful it would be to be saved! I don't like to be robbing people all the time, and I want my sins forgiven." He got down on his knees in the road and talked to God about it and asked God to save him, and God did.

One day the man who had been a robber met the man who had torn up the Bible. The man who had been a robber was telling the other man how wonderful the Bible is. "No!" the other man said, "That book wouldn't help anybody!"

"It helped you," said the former robber, "because it kept you from being robbed."

I hope the man who had torn up the Bible decided the Bible is a good Book!

SOMETHING TO READ FROM THE BIBLE: II Peter 1:16-21

QUESTIONS:

1. Who saw God make the world?
2. Who is the only One who can tell us what happened?
3. Where does He tell us?
4. Can you tell about something the Bible told was going to happen before it did?

A PRAYER:

Dear Lord Jesus, who knows all things, we thank You that there was never a time when God was not alive. We are glad that He knows all things and that He has told us in the Bible the things about heaven that we need to know. We thank You that the Bible is true. Help us to read it and to understand it and to do what it tells us. We ask this in Jesus' name. Amen.

A HYMN TO SING:

"Wonderful Words of Life"

Sing them over again to me,
Wonderful words of life;
Let me more of their beauty see,
Wonderful words of life.
Words of life and beauty
Teach me faith and duty:
Beautiful words, wonderful words,
Wonderful words of life.

37

What Happens If We Do Not Use Our Bibles?

Is it important for us to read the Bible? Is it important for us to do what it tells us to? Oh, yes, it is, but do you know that there are people who think they do not need to read the Bible and obey it? They think that they can find out by themselves all they need to know. They do not understand how little they can find out about God just by thinking about Him. Do you think they would ever know, unless they read the Bible, how much God hates their sins? Would they know that Jesus loves them and died for their sins unless they read it in the Bible? Someone else might read it to them or tell them about it, but they could only find out these things from the Bible.

Of course we can know some things about God by just looking at the flowers and the leaves and the trees. They tell us how wonderful He is, and the sun and the moon and the stars tell us how powerful and glorious He is. But we cannot know how much He loves us except from His telling us about it in the Bible.

We must be careful to read all of the Bible and obey all that it says. We need to notice as we read the Bible that some parts are written for people who lived long ago. For instance, some parts of the Bible were written to tell the people of Israel about building altars and sacrificing or killing cows and other animals on them; if they did these things, God covered over their sins. Today we do not need to sacrifice animals because the Lord Jesus Christ who is the Lamb of God was sacrificed for us once and for all when He died on the cross. We do not need any other sacrifices. But even though the parts of the Bible telling us about these things are not for us today, still it is very helpful and important to read these parts because they tell us so much about God's plan, and His love, and about Jesus. So *all* the Bible is important for us to read and study.

The Bible is all true, and we need to notice what we are to learn from the part we read each day.

But on the other hand we must be very careful not to read some part of the Bible and think, "Oh, surely that cannot be written for me. That is too hard to do. It must be for somebody else, and I don't need to obey it." If it is written for you, obey it whether or not you like to, because it is your job to obey God and do what He tells you in the Bible. You must be very careful not to try to think that the Bible says things that it doesn't intend; and must be careful not to refuse anything that it does say. We may not add anything to the Bible nor take any part of it away.

A poor woman who sold fruit and vegetables was a Christian and loved her Bible. She sat at her fruit and vegetable stand waiting for customers, and while she was waiting, she would read her Bible. One day a man said to her, "What are you reading there?"

"It is the Word of God," she said.

"The Word of God! Who told you that?"

"He told me so Himself."

"Have you ever spoken with Him then? Can you prove that?"

The poor woman felt a little embarrassed. She was not used to talking about the Bible, but at last she said, looking up, "Can you prove to me that there is a sun up in the sky?"

"Why, yes," he said, "the best proof is that it warms me and that I can see its light."

"So it is with me," the woman replied joyously, "the proof of this Book's being the Word of God is that it makes me warm and happy down inside my soul."

SOMETHING TO READ FROM THE BIBLE: Psalm 119:9-16

QUESTIONS:

1. What are some things we can know about God without reading our Bibles?

2. What very important thing does the Bible tell us that we could not find out about God except by reading the Bible?

3. Should we obey the parts of the Bible that tell us to kill animals when we sin? Why don't we need to do this anymore?

4. Why is it important for us to read these parts of the Bible?

Dear Lord Jesus, we thank You so very much for Your holy Word, the Bible. Thank you for telling us in it how we can have our sins forgiven. Please help us to read it every day and to obey it. This we ask in Jesus' name. Amen.

A SONG TO SING:

> The B-I-B-L-E,
> Yes that's the Book for me,
> I'll read and pray and then obey
> The B-I-B-L-E.

38

What Does God Want Me to Do?

WE HAVE ALREADY learned that the most important thing a child can do is to obey God. That is the only way he can really be happy.

Perhaps you are wondering, "How can I know what things God wants me to do?" To find out what God wants you to do, you must ask Him. But will He give you an answer? Yes, indeed, He will be glad to tell you. Perhaps it will seem hard at first to know how to ask Him and how to hear His answer. It isn't like asking Daddy or Mother for something. Yes, we can see them and hear them speak. But we cannot see God and we cannot hear the sound of His voice. So how can we tell what He wants?

This is not such a hard question when we think about it for a little while. Can you think of a way we can find out things from people who live a long way from us? Remember, we said that one way is to get letters from them. The mailman brings the letters, and we read them, and then we know what the other person is thinking, and we can know whether he wants us to do anything for him.

God has written us a long letter. The Bible is God's letter. When we read it, we find that it is not like most letters. It is much longer and tells about many different things. And it tells us hundreds of things God wants us to do or things He doesn't want us to do.

That is why it is so important for us to read our Bibles.

There is another way God helps us to know what He wants. God wants us to do right things and not things that are naughty. Usually we can tell without very much trouble whether a thing is good or bad.

God has given us a feeling deep down inside of us that feels bad and unhappy when we think about wrong things and when we do wrong things. So if you are thinking about doing something and you have that bad feeling, it is God speaking to you and telling you not to do it. Sometimes we say that the feeling is God's voice in our hearts. Sometimes we call it our conscience.

Another way to know about obeying God and what He wants us to do is by asking Mother or Daddy and then obeying.

You can be sure of this, that if you are a Christian, loving the Lord Jesus, and if you want to obey God and do what He wants, then God will help you find out His wishes.

A little boy wanted to do God's will. He wanted to grow up

to be just what God wanted Him to be. He thought that God wanted him to be a doctor or a fireman. He decided to ask God about it. He prayed and asked God to help him find out. God heard the little boy's prayer, but He didn't send an angel to tell him. No, instead He let the little boy think about it for several years while he was going to school, and the more the little boy thought and prayed about it, the more he was sure that God wanted him to be a doctor and then go out and be a missionary. God made him want to do that more than anything else. God was speaking to the boy through his own mind.

Sometimes God may speak to you that way. He does not need to send an angel, but He can help you decide what is best, and what you decide will be God's plan.

SOMETHING TO READ FROM THE BIBLE: Genesis 24:34-48

QUESTIONS:
1. What would you like God to tell you about?
2. Will God need to send an angel to tell you?
3. What are some of the ways that He can make known His will to you?
4. Does God always hear us when we pray?

A PRAYER:
Almighty God and Father of those who put their trust in Your Son Jesus, we thank You that You give the answers to their questions to those who ask You for wisdom. We thank You that You gladly show us Your will. Help us as children to find Your will for our lives. In Jesus' name. Amen.

"Take the Name of Jesus with You"

Precious name, oh, how sweet!
Hope of earth and joy of heaven;
Precious name, oh, how sweet!
Hope of earth and joy of heaven.

39

Why Do Christians Disagree?

A MOTHER SAID to her two children, "Please go down and buy me a loaf of bread while I go out into the garden and work." The children happily jumped on their bicycles and went to the store. But just as they were getting ready to buy the bread, they began to argue. One of them thought that Mother wanted a loaf of brown bread and the other thought that she wanted white bread; one of them thought that she wanted a large loaf and the other thought she wanted a small loaf. The children quarreled so much that all the people in the store were surprised and sorry.

That is a little bit like what happens about some of the

things in the Bible. The Bible tells us, for instance, that Christians should be baptized. But just what does it mean to be baptized? Different Christians think different things about what it means. Some think that the little babies should be baptized, and some think that only older boys and girls and mothers and fathers should be baptized after they are old enough to know about the Lord Jesus and have asked Him to be their Saviour. Some people think that the baptizing should be done by water being sprinkled or poured over the person's head, but other people think that the person's whole body should go under the water.

In the same way there are differences of opinion about how we ought to remember about Jesus' dying for us when we have the Lord's Supper, or Communion, as it is sometimes called.

And so people who believe these different things often need different churches which have different names such as Baptist or Presbyterian or Methodist or Plymouth Brethren or Episcopalian or Bible Church or Lutheran or Pentecostal, Holiness, or Assemblies of God, or many, many other names.

All of these different ideas cannot be right. Some of these people are wrong in what they think God wants.

But in all of these different kinds of churches there is one main thing that all of us who are Christians believe, and that is that the Lord Jesus is the only One who can forgive our sins and save us forever. That is the most important thing.

So you see, these different churches are made up of people who love the Lord. And all those who love the Lord, even though they may not agree on what the Bible teaches about many things, belong to Him. The one thing they do understand is God's love, that He has made it possible for them to have their sins forgiven, and they have accepted Him as their Saviour.

I am sorry to say, though, that there are some churches that do not believe very much of the Bible and do not agree with other Christians even on the important things. Of course, these are not true churches, even though they are called by that name, and most of the people in such churches are not Christians at all, because they do not understand about Jesus' dying for them.

Sometimes people who go to churches where the Lord Jesus is loved say they are Christians, but don't really love Him at all. They do not understand God's forgiveness through Jesus Christ's death, but they enjoy the church because their fathers or mothers were members and because they think that it may help them get to heaven. We need to pray for such people and try to help them understand more about God's way of salvation.

During the visit of the king of Italy to one of his cities many years ago, the nine Protestant ministers of that city asked if they might visit him. The young king was glad to have them do this but was very much surprised when he met them to find that one was a Methodist, another a Baptist, a third a Presbyterian, and so on.

"I do not understand," said the king, "how you can all be ministers of the same gospel and yet have so many distinctions."

One of the ministers replied, "In your army there are many regiments where a different uniform is called by different names but they are all under one comander-in-chief and follow one flag. In the same way we are divided into various churches but we know only one Chief—Jesus Christ—and we follow but one banner, that of the gospel of our crucified and risen Lord."

The king said, "Thank you for this good explanation. You

have made me understand that while there are differences among you on the small matters there is agreement on the most important things."

SOMETHING TO READ FROM THE BIBLE: Romans 14:1-13

QUESTIONS:

1. Why did the children quarrel?
2. What are some things Christians do not agree about?
3. What is the important thing that all real Christians do agree about?
4. What is a Christian?

A PRAYER:

Almighty Father in heaven, we thank You that You are full of kindness toward those who want to obey You. Help us to find out what is right from the Bible and help us to be kind to other Christians who do not understand things as we do. In Jesus' name. Amen.

A SONG TO SING:

Into my heart, into my heart,
Come into my heart, Lord Jesus;
Come in today,
Come in to stay,
Come into my heart, Lord Jesus.

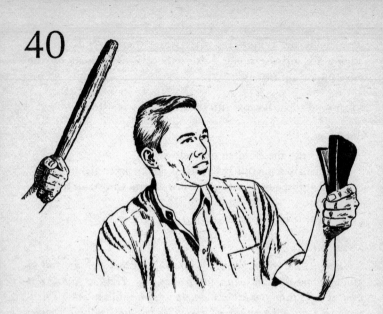

40

What It Means to Forgive

JESUS TELLS US to forgive people who try to hurt us and don't like us.

To forgive someone means that we should not be angry with those who have done something wrong to us or hurt us.

If someone hits you, will you hit him back? Not if you forgive him. If you forgive him, you will smile and turn away instead of hitting him back. The Bible tells us again and again to forgive people who try to hurt us.

Jesus tells us that God our Father is kind to those who are His enemies and we should be kind to our enemies too.

One day a missionary was preaching on a street corner to people who didn't know about the Lord Jesus and didn't love

Him at all. One of the men sneaked behind the missionary and hit him on the head with a large stick and knocked him down. The other people listening thought this was not fair, and they grabbed the man with the stick and called a policeman to take him to jail, but the missionary said, "No."

All the people were very much surprised. "He has hurt you," they said, "now he is to be hurt."

"No," said the missionary, "because Jesus, the One I am telling you about, told me to be kind to those who hurt me and to forgive them." Then the missionary turned to the man who had hit him and said, "I forgive you, but always remember that you owe your escape to Jesus who told me not to be angry with you."

So the policeman let the man go.

The people who were watching could hardly believe it. They thought Jesus must be a very wonderful Person, and they were glad to hear more about Him from the missionary.

What if the missionary had become angry with the man? Probably the people wouldn't have listened as well after that. They would have thought it didn't help a person to be a Christian, because he became as angry as other people.

When someone hurts you, do you know now what is the best thing to do? If someone says something about you that isn't nice, what can you do? It is easy to become angry about it, but Jesus can help you not to mind; instead, you can smile about it if you think about Jesus often during the day. He is with us all the time and we can talk to Him. He makes us happy, so we don't get angry with people He loves, even when they aren't nice to us.

SOMETHING TO READ FROM THE BIBLE: Matthew 18:21-35

1. If someone hurts us, what is the best way to hurt them back?
2. If we forgive someone, will we want to hurt him for what he has done to us?
3. How many sins has Jesus forgiven us for?

A PRAYER:

Our heavenly Father, we thank You for the forgiveness of our sins, that You have forgiven so many of them. Help us now to forgive those who try to hurt us and to love them and help them come to know You. In Jesus' name. Amen.

A HYMN TO SING:

> God will take care of you,
> Through every day,
> O'er all the way;
> He will take care of you,
> God will take care of you.

41

A Prize for You in Heaven

Do YOU LIKE to win prizes? Have you ever been in a race at a Sunday school picnic, or at school when ribbons were given to those who won?

Have you heard about a prize that Jesus is going to give you? Now don't ask me what the prize is going to be, because I don't know. It is going to be a surprise—a very wonderful surprise from God Himself for His dear child.

But I can tell you how to get the prize. We earn the prize or reward by the good and kind things that we, as Christians, do while we are here on earth. Whenever Christian boys and girls help Mother and Daddy, God prepares a reward for them. But whenever we disobey Mother or Daddy, or are unkind, or do other wrong things, then God is grieved with us.

How important it is, the way we live down here! We live here in this world for only a few years. Perhaps it seems a long time to think of living for sixty or seventy years, but it is not very long when we think how long "forever" is, and that God's children will be with Him in heaven forever. The reward God is getting ready for you is one that will last always and always and will make you very happy. How sad it will be if you get to heaven and find that your reward is very small! Then you would wish and wish that you could come back to earth and try for a better prize. Then it will be too late, but it is not too late now; you have your whole life ahead of you now, and you can spend it all for the Lord Jesus. How happy you will be then, when you get to heaven, that you have decided now when you are still young to live your life for Jesus!

Once a man visited in the home of a friend so that they could talk together about their work. The two men went into a room where two other men were sitting quietly at a table. The man who was visiting and his friend talked about their work for a long, long time. Finally, when they had said everything that they wanted to, the man who owned the house said to his friend, "Whenever I talk with anyone about my work, I have people listening to the conversation and writing down everything that is said. These two men sitting at the table have been writing down everything I said and everything you said, and now we will ask them to read back to us all that we discussed so that there will be no misunderstanding."

The man who had come to visit was very, very much surprised. He did not know that the two men were writing down everything. If he had known that, he would have been more careful about what he said, because he would not want other people to read some of the things. But then it was too late. He had already said them.

When we reach heaven, the books will be opened in which will be written all the things that we have said and done. Jesus will decide what He can reward us for. And do you know, there will be some surprises? Some people who thought they had done a lot for God will find it didn't count very much because they didn't love God very much. And some people will get a much greater prize than they expect.

We do not know just what the judgment will be like, but we do know that we will be given prizes, and that we must be careful how we live now so that we will have prizes then.

SOMETHING TO READ FROM THE BIBLE: I Corinthians 3:11-17

QUESTIONS:

1. What kind of reward will we be given when we get to heaven?
2. Who will give us the reward?
3. How will it be decided how big a reward we should have?
4. Have you done anything today that would help your reward, or hurt it?

A PRAYER:

Dear Lord Jesus, we thank You for all that you are getting ready for us there in heaven. Help us to love and obey You so that we can honor You. May we think often of all that You want to give us. In Your name. Amen.

A HYMN TO SING:

When we all get to heaven,
What a day of rejoicing that will be!
When we all see Jesus,
We'll sing and shout the victory.

42

The Lord's Day

SUNDAY IS REALLY a very special day. God gave it to us as a time of rest from many of the jobs we need to do all the other days. On Sunday we don't need to go to school, and Dad doesn't usually need to go to work. Instead, we can go to Sunday school and church and join our friends in praising God together for all His loving-kindness to us. How much harder it would be to remember to worship God as we should if we did not have our pastor to help us in the church services on Sunday. God wants us to meet with other Christians and sing and speak His praises together. That is one of the best things for us to do on Sunday. It is also a time when Mother and Dad can often spend more time than usual with the children and read some extra stories when all the family can be to-gether.

Sunday is not a day for "having fun." It is a day for taking special time to thank and worship God and to remember Him. That is not easy to do if we spend the day working or even playing. When God made the world and everything else, He used six days, and the Bible tells us He rested on the seventh day, and made it especially holy. The Jewish people used this seventh day for their worship and ceremonies in the temple. God commanded them to "Remember the sabbath day to keep it holy." Most Christians set aside Sunday, the first day of each week, the day on which the Lord Jesus arose from the dead, as a day when we can come together to praise and worship God.

One Sunday afternoon a minister was walking home from church, which was far from his house. A little boy came along the road carrying a rake. Farther on a man in working clothes came along and asked the minister, "Have you seen my little boy walking along this way?"

"Was he carrying a rake?" asked the minister.

"Yes, that's he," said the man.

"A little boy with a bad memory?" asked the minister.

The little boy's father was surprised. "Well," he said, "I don't think he has a bad memory. He doesn't forget things very often. What makes you think he has a bad memory?"

"Oh, I know he has," said the minister, "and I think he be-longs to a family that has poor memories."

"Why, what in the world makes you think that?" asked the boy's father.

"Because," said the minister, "he has forgotten to remember the Sabbath day to keep it holy."

Then the minister explained to him that God has given one

153

day in every seven for rest and praise and worship for all that God has done for us.

SOMETHING TO READ FROM THE BIBLE: Isaiah 58:13-14

QUESTIONS:

1. What is one of the best things for us to do on Sunday?
2. Is Sunday the only day we should thank and worship God and remember Him?
3. Can you think of a reason why God wants us to rest on Sunday?

A PRAYER:

We thank You, our heavenly Father, for giving us Sunday as a special day. Help us to remember to keep it holy and to love You more. In Jesus' name. Amen.

A HYMN TO SING:

> O worship the King, all glorious above,
> And gratefully sing His power and His love;
> Our Shield and Defender, the Ancient of Days,
> Pavilioned in splendor, and girded with praise.

Are You Angry with God?

THERE IS A BIG, HARD WORD in the Bible called "reconciliation," and I am going to tell you what it means. It means that you have been angry with someone, but now the quarrel is ended and you are happy again. If some other child should break one of your toys, you would be very sorry or angry, but if the child said that he was sorry, then you would forgive him, and you could play happily with him again. When that happens, we say that you have been reconciled to the child who broke your toy.

But wouldn't it be strange if the child who broke your toy was still angry and quarrelsome about it after you had forgiven him? You would think that he would be very happy, but sometimes it happens that you can be happy toward some-

155

one who has hurt you but that person isn't happy toward you. You love him, but he doesn't love you, even though you are the one he has hurt and you have forgiven him.

That is the way it is between a boy or a girl who is not a Christian, and God. Because of the many wrong things the child has done, God has been angry. But then the Lord Jesus came and died and God could forgive that child. God didn't need to be angry with him anymore. God is reconciled to the child.

But the trouble is that the child is not reconciled to God. The child is still disobedient and not on friendly terms with God even though God wants to forgive him. He still wants to quarrel with God by doing and saying what he pleases.

Perhaps the child doesn't realize that he really doesn't like God. If he loved God, then he wouldn't keep doing things God doesn't like.

What needs to be done is for the child who is not a Christian to admit that he has done many wrong things and to ask God to forgive him for Jesus' sake. When the boy or girl does that, he finds he no longer disagrees or quarrels with God. God already loves him and now the child loves God and is finally happy. He has become reconciled to God.

A little girl said, "Mother, am I a Christian? Can I tell by the way I feel?"

"Well," replied her mother, "suppose you tell me how you feel."

Her little girl smiled and said, "You know how it is when you have quarreled with a person and it is all made up, how happy you feel? Well, it seems like I have been angry with God for a long time, but it is all made up now, and I feel so very happy."

156

That little girl had become reconciled to God. Are you reconciled to God?

SOMETHING TO READ FROM THE BIBLE: II Corinthians 5:17-21

QUESTIONS:

1. What does reconciliation mean?
2. When does God want to forgive your sins?
3. What do we need to do to be forgiven?
4. Have you been reconciled to God?

A PRAYER:

Dear Father in heaven, how sad it is that we have been quarreling and angry with You when You have been so kind to us. Forgive us for our foolish ways and help us to love You, because You have loved us so much. In Jesus' name we ask it. Amen.

A HYMN TO SING:

Since Jesus came into my heart,
Since Jesus came into my heart,
Floods of joy o'er my soul like the sea billows roll,
Since Jesus came into my heart.

44

Going to Sunday School

WHY IS IT IMPORTANT for us to go to Sunday school and church every week?

It is important because God wants us to be with other Christians and talk with them about God and all that He has done for us, and to worship Him together. God tells us in the Bible not to forget to do this. If we forget and don't go to Sunday school and church, it is harder for us to keep loving Jesus as much as we should. God has made us so that we need help from each other.

When you go to Sunday school, then, it is important to remember that God is asking you to go there so that you can help your friends love Him more. You will learn more about Jesus when you go, but you should not go just to be helped, but to help others. This means of course that you must be very careful about what you do in Sunday school. You must be very careful to respect the teacher, and to be careful about unnecessary noise, because you are in the place where God is and you have come there to worship Him and learn about your great Saviour.

It is also a wonderful thing to get boys and girls who do not know about the Lord Jesus to come with you to Sunday school. Do you have any little neighbor next door, or down the street, who doesn't seem to know very much about the Lord Jesus? Perhaps you can ask him to come to Sunday school with you, and that will be one of the ways he can find out about how much God loves him.

Church time is different from Sunday school and requires a lot of sitting still! Sometimes children find that it is hard work to sit still and listen because it is not easy to understand what the minister is talking about. But it is good practice to listen and enjoy the things you can understand, then think about them.

A good way to get ready for church and Sunday school is to think about it before you go there. If you remember on Saturday that "tomorrow is Sunday and I get to go to Sunday school and church," then you can pray about it and ask God to help you to learn more about Him; then you will be more ready to go and worship Him when the time comes on Sunday morning, and it won't be so hard to sit still!

The story is told about a little boy who decided that he didn't want to go to Sunday school anymore. Instead, he played with his toys and with some other children in the neighborhood. After a while the little boy forgot that God loved him and was watching over him, and the little boy and his friends stole a bicycle that they saw in a yard. Someone saw them taking the bicycle and called the police. The little boy was taken to the judge, and the judge talked to him. Do you know what the judge said? He told the little boy that he ought to begin going to Sunday school again right away.

"If you don't," the judge said, "you will probably steal other things and then we will have to put you in jail. But if you go to Sunday school you will learn about God and you won't want to steal because He doesn't want you to."

Years later when the little boy had become a big man he met the judge again. "Judge," he said, "I am very grateful for what you told me that day. I did go back to Sunday school and I took the Lord Jesus as my Saviour. If you hadn't talked to me like that I might be in jail today."

I am sure that the little boy was glad most of all because at Sunday school he found Jesus.

SOMETHING TO READ FROM THE BIBLE: Hebrews 10:24-25

QUESTIONS:

1. Can you name two reasons for going to Sunday school?
2. How does it help other children in your Sunday school class when you are there?
3. Why does it help to think on Saturday about going to Sunday school?
4. Should we go to Sunday school if we are not quiet and respectful to our teachers?

A PRAYER:

Our Father, we thank You that there are so many other Christians for us to talk with. We thank You for our Sunday school teachers and the pastor of our church. Bless them and help them as they are preparing to teach us next Sunday morning. Help us to enjoy what is said and to understand what You are telling us through them. *In Jesus' name.*

A HYMN TO SING:

> Tell me the story of Jesus,
> Write on my heart ev'ry word;
> Tell me the story most precious,
> Sweetest that ever was heard.

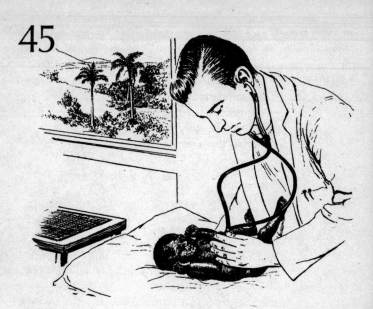

45

What Are You Going to Be When You Grow Up?

HAVE YOU EVER WONDERED what you ought to be when you get big? There are so many things you could be that probably you have wondered how to decide which is best. You could be a doctor, or a farmer, or a teacher, or a typist—or hundreds of other things. But there is Someone who knows just exactly what you ought to be. That Someone is God, and He will gladly tell you what you should be when it is the right time for you to know. So you don't need to worry about it!

How will God tell you? There are many ways that He can speak to you. One of the ways is by the abilities He gives you. Some boys are very good ball players and some are not. Some girls are good at singing and some aren't good singers at all. If God has made you so you aren't good at playing ball, then probably He doesn't want you to spend your life as a ball player! But perhaps instead He has made you so that you are a very good musician and can play the piano, or violin or trumpet. Or perhaps He has made you so that after you have gone to school enough you will be able to do all the things a doctor can, or a farmer. If you discover that God has made you so you would like to be a farmer, but you wouldn't at all enjoy being a doctor, then that is one of the ways you will know that God probably doesn't want you to be a doctor.

It is a good idea to think about the many kinds of work there are to do and then think about which you would like; as you become bigger it is quite probable that one thing in particular will be just what you would want to do. God will make you know whether it is the right thing for you if you ask Him to.

Some boys and girls seem to know all the time just what they want to be when they are older, but others don't know until many years have gone by and they have finished school. Sometimes God wants people to wait until they are grown up before He tells them.

If you want God to show you, then you can be sure that He will. When the right time comes, you will know, if you are trusting Him.

A boy who was only six years old said to his father, "Daddy, I am going to be a doctor when I grow up and I am going to be a missionary. I am going to go to Tibet and help the people there know about the Lord Jesus."

"That's fine," his father said.

As the years went by the boy grew up and went through high school, then college and then on to medical school where he learned how to be a good doctor and surgeon.

When he had become a doctor he tried to go to the land of Tibet, but the Lord told him to go to Africa instead. He is in Africa now helping the people there to be well, but he is doing more than that. He is helping them to be well in their hearts and souls by knowing about Jesus. When he is giving them medicine he talks to them about his Lord, and many of them accept Jesus as their Saviour.

SOMETHING TO READ FROM THE BIBLE: I Corinthians 12:12-31

QUESTIONS:

1. How does God help us find out what He wants us to be?
2. Will God let us make a mistake if we ask Him for help?
3. How can we find out what different kinds of work are like?

A PRAYER:

Lord Jesus, I know that You have a particular job for me to do, and I want to do it for You. Please show me just what I'm to be when I grow up. I don't need to know now, but when it is time for me to know, I am trusting You to make me understand.

A HYMN TO SING:

> Work, for the night is coming,
> Work through the morning hours;
> Work while the dew is sparkling;
> Work 'mid springing flowers.
> Work when the day grows brighter,
> Work in the glowing sun;
> Work, for the night is coming,
> When man's work is done.

46

Who May Talk to God?

IF YOU WERE VISITING in Washington, D.C., and wanted to talk with the President of the United States, do you think that you could just walk into the White House and start talking to him?

No, of course not. You would need a special invitation, because the President is far too busy to talk with all the people who would like to visit with him. It is a great privilege to be able to talk to the President of the United States, and there are very few people who are able to do it.

God is so much greater than the President of the United States that we would think no one could *ever* talk to Him. Yet, strange to say, God is glad to have us come and is always ready to give us an invitation whenever we want one.

Wouldn't it be exciting to visit with the One who made

you? Wouldn't it be wonderful to be able to talk with Someone who could tell you everything that you need to know, and
help you in every way? I am sure that you would be very
much excited if you had an invitation to talk with Someone
like that. And yet that is just the way it is with God. He is the
One who has made everything and has put the stars away up
there in the sky and is willing to make your life good and use-
ful. But He is never too busy to welcome you.

You may have this exciting and wonderful experience of
talking with God!

If you would like to make this visit, you may do so now.
Close your eyes and bow your head and think about God and
how much He loves you. Then speak to Him about many
things. First you can thank Him for being so kind to you.
Thank Him for sending the Lord Jesus to die for your sins.
Thank Him for warm clothing, and for your parents and family. Thank Him because you have the opportunity of going to
school when many children in other lands are not able to do
that.

And then perhaps you would want to ask Him for some
things, for He is glad to have you bring your questions and
requests. Ask Him to bless Mother and Daddy and take care
of the missionaries and to help them in their work.

Will God hear you? Yes, indeed! He is right here in the
room and He knows everything you say. He also knows all
that you are thinking. You don't even need to say the words
out loud when you are talking to God, because He can hear
you when you speak in your heart.

Jesus loves to have His children come and talk with Him.
He is your Father and your Friend, so talk to Him and tell
Him all your needs and troubles, and thank Him for being
so good to you.

A boy named John lost his glasses one day and couldn't find them anywhere. He looked on the dresser in his room and he looked under the davenport downstairs and they weren't there. He looked on a shelf where he sometimes kept his things and he looked in a drawer that was full of his papers and his pencils and toys, but the glasses weren't there.

His sister Catherine said, "I know Somebody who knows where your glasses are, John."

"Who?" John wanted to know. "Is it you? Have you been hiding them?"

"No," Catherine said, "but God knows just where they are. He sees them. Maybe you could ask Him to tell you and then you could find them."

"It's a good idea," John said. "Will you help me to talk to Him?"

So the two children kneeled down and prayed. John said, "Lord Jesus, You know where my glasses are and I don't. Would You please help me find them?"

And Catherine said, "Lord Jesus, You are looking right at John's glasses now; and You could tell us so we can see them too. Please help us to find John's glasses."

Two weeks went by and still the glasses were gone. "I guess we'll have to get another pair," Mother said sadly. "I hope they won't cost too much."

That afternoon when the children were out playing in the garage, Cathy and John decided that they would climb up and sit on a shelf that hung out over where the car was parked when Daddy brought it home at night. It was hard to climb up so they decided to use Daddy's stepladder. They put the ladder in place and climbed up, and there were John's glasses lying there in the dust on the shelf!

This is a true story except for the names of the children

and one or two other details. How the glasses got there no one ever knew. But God knew just where they were, and He showed the children.

SOMETHING TO READ FROM THE BIBLE: Hebrews 4:16

QUESTIONS:

1. Can we go and talk with the President whenever we wish to?
2. Name some of the ways that God is greater than the President or anyone else.
3. How often may we come and talk with God? Why?
4. What are some of the things that we should talk to God about?

A PRAYER:

Lord Jesus, we thank You that we may come at any time to talk with You about our problems. Teach us to pray and help us to remember how great You are and how kind. We thank You in Jesus' name. Amen.

A HYMN TO SING:

Sweet hour of prayer, sweet hour of prayer,
That calls me from a world of care,
And bids me at my Father's throne
Make all my wants and wishes known;
In seasons of distress and grief,
My soul has often found relief,
And oft escaped the tempter's snare,
By thy return, sweet hour of prayer.

47

Who Made Everything?

DID YOU EVER make things out of clay or mud? Sometimes it is fun trying to mold clay to look just like real houses or dogs. But did you ever try to make a real dog out of the clay? Of course you could never do that. Only God can make things that are alive. No one has ever been able to make a living thing except God.

How did life begin? Where did the first dog come from? How did the world get here? The Bible tells us very simply that God made these things and gave them to us.

And yet there are people who are very intelligent who say they don't know how the world got here. They say God didn't make life. It just happened, they say. They think that millions of years ago a tiny thing too small to see suddenly became alive and began to grow. It was not God who made it become alive they say, because there is no God! What a strange thing to say! These people say they don't know how life began except they say they know God didn't do it! Although they are wise in some ways, they are very foolish when it comes to knowing how things began.

The Bible tells us that after God made the world, He took the dust from the ground and formed it into a man's body and then breathed into it the breath of life.

God alone can give this life.

Two friends named Mr. Jones and Mr. Smith were walking along the beach in the wet sand. Mr. Jones said, "I don't believe that we can ever know for sure whether or not God made the world." Just then they came to a footprint in the sand. "Someone has been walking along here this morning," Mr. Jones said.

"Oh?" said Mr. Smith. "How can you be so sure?"

"Well, don't be silly," Mr. Jones exclaimed; "here are someone's footprints, so somebody must have been here to make the footprints."

"Just so," said Mr. Smith. "And we can know that the world was made by God because the trees and the flowers and the sunshine and the rain are His footprints to tell us that He has been here."

SOMETHING TO READ FROM THE BIBLE: Genesis 1:1-23

QUESTIONS:

1. Has anyone ever been able to make a living person?
2. How did the stars get into the sky?
3. Why do you think that some men don't want to believe that God made them?

A PRAYER:

Our Father in heaven, we thank You that You made the stars and everything that is good. We thank You for giving us our bodies and our lives. We thank You for letting us come and live with You in heaven always, and for Jesus who made this possible. In Jesus' name.

A HYMN TO SING:

> Praise God from whom all blessings flow;
> Praise Him, all creatures here below;
> Praise Him above, ye heavenly host;
> Praise Father, Son, and Holy Ghost.

48

Telling Lies

DOES IT SURPRISE YOU to know that there is something that God hates? We usually think of God as a God of love, and He is. But He also hates lies. So you and I had better not ever have anything to do with lying.

God wants His sons and daughters to be absolutely truthful and honest. He does not want them to be tricky and slippery. He wants them to be boys and girls whose word can be depended upon. He wants boys and girls who, when they say they are going to do something, will do it; if they say that they won't tell a secret, then they won't, no matter how much somebody begs them to.

But if we always tell the truth won't we sometimes get into trouble? Yes, of course we will! If you do something wrong and then when you are asked about it, admit that you did it, you are apt to be punished. But it is very, very much better to be punished for doing wrong than it is to tell a lie. If you tell a lie, you will have done two wrong things instead of only one, and God must punish you for both of them. Being punished by God for two things is far, far worse than punished by our parents for one thing.

What's more, boys and girls who are known always to tell the truth no matter what happens to them, are the boys and girls who grow up to be men and women who are trusted by others. Other people find out they are honest and give them big jobs to do because everyone knows that they will not cheat.

A boy named Jack wanted to go to a Christian summer camp and didn't have enough money. He decided that he would get the money by telling a lie. He went to the pastor of his church and said, "Pastor Smith, my uncle sent me some money so that I could go to the camp next week and the money got lost in the mail and it hasn't come."

"Oh, that's too bad," said Pastor Smith. "Perhaps we can find some money somewhere, enough so that you can go to camp. It is too bad for you not to be able to go just because the money was lost in the mail."

The pastor talked to someone about sending the boy to camp, and the money was given. So the boy went to camp the next week. But for some reason he was very unhappy. Whenever it was time to pray he didn't feel like praying and even when it was time to play he didn't feel like playing. The trouble was that he was a Christian and he had told a lie, and God hates lies. God was already punishing him by making him dreadfully unhappy. Finally he felt so badly that the people in charge of the camp thought that he ought to go home because he was sick.

When they had taken him home, his pastor came to visit him.

"I am sorry that you are sick, Jack," the pastor said.

Then Jack began to cry. He told the pastor what had happened and how he had told a lie. The pastor was surprised, and sorry that Jack had done such a thing. Then Jack said something that was very true.

"Pastor Smith," he said, "God didn't need me to tell lies for Him in order to help Him get me to camp. He could have sent the money some other way if He had wanted me to go and if I had asked Him. I'm sorry that I told you the lie."

"You are right," the pastor said. "The Lord never wants that kind of help."

The next year Jack went to camp, but he didn't tell a lie to get there. He worked hard during the year and saved enough money and had a very good time at camp. Jack decided that he never wanted to tell another lie.

SOMETHING TO READ FROM THE BIBLE: Ephesians 4:25;
    Colossians 3:9; John 8:44

QUESTIONS:
1. Who is it who likes to hear boys and girls telling lies?
2. Sometimes people get things by lying and other people never find out about it. Do you think that in some cases it pays to lie? Why, or why not?
3. Will God forgive us if we have told a lie? What should we do?

A PRAYER:

O God, our heavenly Father, we confess that we have done many wrong things and we have told lies. We are sorry and we pray You will help us always to tell the truth even though it may be hard to do. We thank You for this help. In Jesus' name. Amen.

A HYMN TO SING:

"True-Hearted, Whole-Hearted"

Peal out the watchword! Silence it never!
Song of our spirits, rejoicing and free;
Peal out the watchword! loyal forever,
King of our lives, by Thy grace we will be.

Moody Press, a ministry of the Moody Bible Institute, is designed for education, evangelization and edification. If we may assist you in knowing more about Christ and the Christian life, please write us without obligation to: Moody Press, c/o MLM, Chicago, Illinois 60610.